CLASSIC ROCK

**MELODY LINE, CHORDS AND LYRICS
FOR KEYBOARD • GUITAR • VOCAL**

HAL•LEONARD

0-7935-4653-2

HAL•LEONARD™
CORPORATION
7777 W. BLUEMOUND RD. P.O. BOX 13819 MILWAUKEE, WI 53213

Welcome to the PAPERBACK SONGS SERIES.

Do you play piano, guitar, electronic keyboard, sing or play any instrument for that matter? If so, this handy "pocket tune" book is for you.

The concise, one-line music notation consists of:

MELODY, LYRICS & CHORD SYMBOLS

Whether strumming the chords on guitar, "faking" an arrangement on piano/keyboard or singing the lyrics, these fake book style arrangements can be enjoyed at any experience level – hobbyist to professional.

The musical skills necessary to successfully use this book are minimal. If you play guitar and need some help with chords, a basic chord chart is included at the back of the book.

While playing and singing is the first thing that comes to mind when using this book, it can also serve as a compact, comprehensive reference guide.

However you choose to use this PAPERBACK SONGS SERIES book, by all means have fun!

CONTENTS

(contents continued)

AMERICAN WOMAN

Words and Music by BURTON CUMMINGS,
RANDY BACHMAN, GARY PETERSON and JIM KALE

'mer - i - can wom - an gon - na

mess _ your mind. _ I say "A," mess _ your mind. _
mm. _

Moderate Rock

(Instrumental)

A - mer - i - can Wom -
A - mer - i - can Wom -

- an, stay a - way from
- an, get a - way from
- an, I said get a -

me. _ A - mer - i - can Wom -
me. _ A - mer - i - can Wom -
way. _ A - mer - i - can Wom -

- an, ma - ma let me be. _
- an, ma - ma let me be. _
- an, lis - ten what I say. _

ADDICTED TO LOVE

Words and Music by
ROBERT PALMER

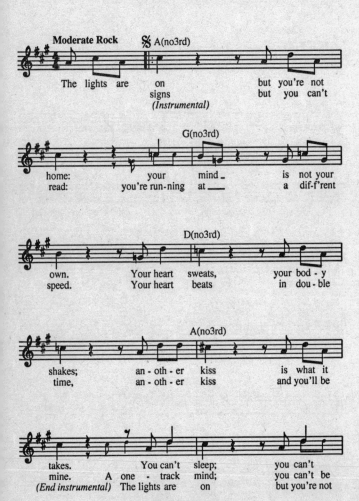

Moderate Rock

A(no3rd)

The lights are on
signs
(Instrumental)

but you're not
but you can't

G(no3rd)

home: your   mind   is not your
read: you're run-ning   at   a   dif-f'rent

D(no3rd)

own.   Your heart   sweats,   your bod - y
speed.   Your heart   beats   in dou - ble

A(no3rd)

shakes;   an - oth - er   kiss   is what it
time,   an - oth - er   kiss   and you'll be

takes.   You can't   sleep;   you can't
mine.   A one - track   mind;   you can't be
(End instrumental) The lights are   on   but you're not

G(no3rd)

eat;   there's no   doubt   you're in
saved;   ob - liv - i - on   is all you
home;   your will   is not your

D(no3rd)

deep.   Your throat is tight,   you can't breathe,
crave.   If there's some   left for
own.   Your heart sweats,   your teeth

A(no3rd)

you,   an - oth - er kiss   is all you
grind,   an - oth - er kiss   and you'll be

F#m   D

need.
do.   Oh, _____ you _____ like to think that you're im -
mine.

A

mune _ to the stuff, oh yeah? _____

F#m   D

It's clos-er _____ to the truth to say you

can't get e - nough; you know you're

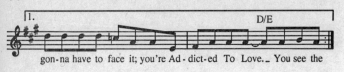

1.

D/E

gon-na have to face it; you're Ad-dict-ed To Love._ You see the

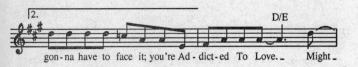

2.

D/E

gon-na have to face it; you're Ad-dict-ed To Love._ Might_

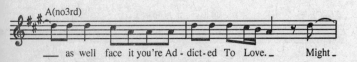

A(no3rd)

___ as well face it you're Ad-dict-ed To Love._ Might_

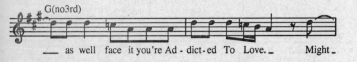

G(no3rd)

___ as well face it you're Ad-dict-ed To Love._ Might_

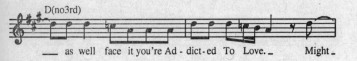

D(no3rd)

___ as well face it you're Ad-dict-ed To Love._ Might_

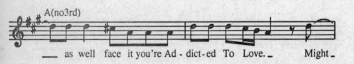

A(no3rd)

___ as well face it you're Ad-dict-ed To Love._ Might_

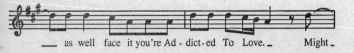

___ as well face it you're Ad-dict-ed To Love._ Might_

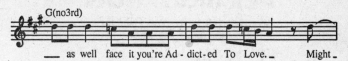

_ as well face it you're Ad - dict - ed To Love. _ Might _

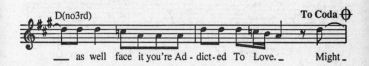

To Coda ⊕

_ as well face it you're Ad - dict - ed To Love. _ Might _

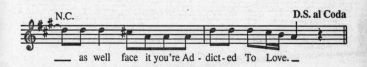

D.S. al Coda

_ as well face it you're Ad - dict - ed To Love. _

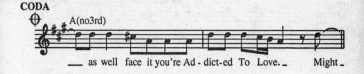

CODA
⊕

_ as well face it you're Ad - dict - ed To Love. _ Might _

_ as well face it, might _ as well face it,

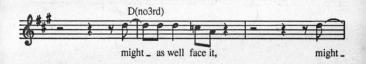

might _ as well face it, might _

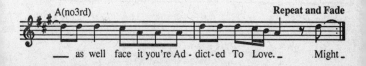

Repeat and Fade

_ as well face it you're Ad - dict - ed To Love. _ Might _

ALL RIGHT NOW

Words and Music by PAUL RODGERS
and ANDY FRASER

ANGIE

Words and Music by MICK JAGGER
and KEITH RICHARDS

An-gie, An-gie, when will those clouds all dis-ap-pear?

An - gie, __

An - gie, where will it lead us from

here? __ With no lov-ing in our souls __ and no

mon-ey in our coats, __ you can't say __ we're sat-is-fied,

but An-gie, An - gie,

you can't say we nev-er tried. __

19

Oh, — An - gie, don't — you weep, all your kiss-

- es still taste sweet, I hate that sad-ness in — your eyes, —

but An-gie,

An - gie, ain't it time — we said good -

bye? _____ (Oh, yes.) *(Instrumental)*

With no lov-ing in our souls — and no

ANOTHER ONE
BITES THE DUST

Words and Music by
JOHN DEACON

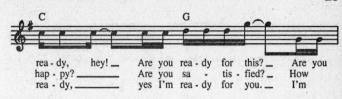

rea - dy, hey! _ Are you rea - dy for this? _ Are you
hap - py? _____ Are you sa - tis - fied? _ How
rea - dy, _____ yes I'm rea - dy for you. _ I'm

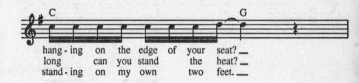

hang - ing on the edge of your seat? _
long can you stand the heat? _
stand - ing on my own two feet. _

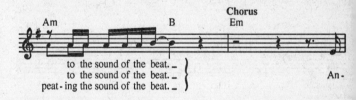

Out of the door - way the bul - lets rip _
Out of the door - way the bul - lets rip _
Out of the door - way the bul - lets rip, _ re -

Chorus

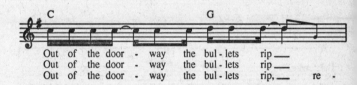

to the sound of the beat. _
to the sound of the beat. _
peat - ing the sound of the beat. _

An-

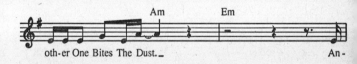

oth - er One Bites The Dust. _

An-

oth - er One Bites The Dust. _ And an -

24

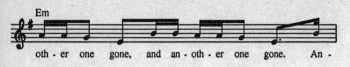

oth - er one gone, and an - oth - er one gone. An -

oth - er One Bites The Dust. _____

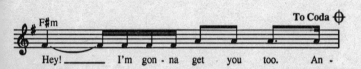

Hey! _____ I'm gon - na get you too. An -

oth - er One Bites The Dust. _

oth - er One Bites The Dust. _

(Hand Clapping)

An -

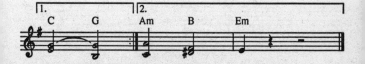

BACK IN THE U.S.S.R.

Words and Music by
JOHN LENNON and PAUL McCARTNEY

BAD CASE OF
LOVING YOU

Words and Music by
MOON MARTIN

30

THE BOYS ARE BACK IN TOWN

Words and Music by
PHILIP PARRIS LYNOTT

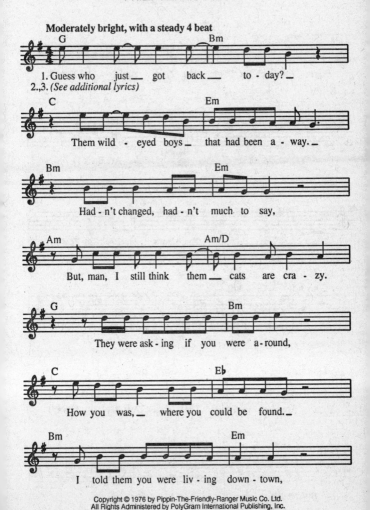

Moderately bright, with a steady 4 beat

1. Guess who just got back to-day?
2.,3. *(See additional lyrics)*

Them wild - eyed boys that had been a - way.

Had - n't changed, had - n't much to say,

But, man, I still think them cats are cra - zy.

They were ask - ing if you were a - round,

How you was, where you could be found.

I told them you were liv - ing down - town,

32

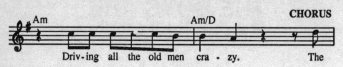

Driv-ing all the old men cra - zy. The

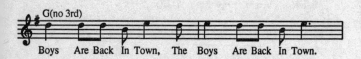

Boys Are Back In Town, The Boys Are Back In Town.

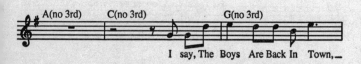

I say, The Boys Are Back In Town, —

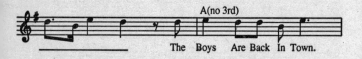

The Boys Are Back In Town.

The Boys Are Back In Town, The Boys Are Back In Town, The

Boys Are Back In Town, The Boys Are Back In Town.

(Instrumental)

INTERLUDE

Spread the word a-round,

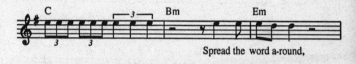

Guess _ who's back in town? _

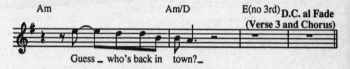

Additional Lyrics

2. You know that chick that used to dance a lot
   Every night she'd be on the floor shaking what she'd got
   Man, when I tell you she was cool, she was hot
   I mean she was steaming

   And that time over at Johnny's place
   Well, this chick got up and she slapped Johnny's face
   Man, we just fell about the place
   if that chick don't wanna know, forget her.
   (Chorus & Interlude)

3. Friday night they'll be dressed to kill
   Down at Dino's Bar and Grill
   The drink will flow and blood will spill
   And if the boys want to fight, you better let 'em.

   That jukebox in the corner blasting out my favorite song
   The nights are getting warmer, it won't be long
   It won't be long till summer comes
   Now that the boys are here again.
   (Chorus and Fade)

BEAST OF BURDEN

Words and Music by MICK JAGGER
and KEITH RICHARDS

E   E/G♯   A

You keep on tell-ing me I ain't your kind of man,_ ain't I

E   B/D♯ C♯m   A

rough e-nough.   Oh!   ain't I

E   B/D♯ C♯m   A

tough e-nough,   ain't I

E   B/D♯ C♯m   A

rich e-nough, in love e-nough,   Ooh ooh_ please.

E   B/D♯ C♯m   A   E

I'll nev-er be your Beast.
I'll nev-er be your Beast.
_ I won't need no Beast_

A   E

_ of Bur - den.   I'll nev-er be your Beast_
_ of Bur - den.   I've walked for miles and my _
_ of Bur - den.   I need no fuss-ing

A   E   B/D♯

_ of Bur - den,   nev-er, nev-er, nev-er, nev-er,
_ feet are hurt - ing,   all I want is
I need no nurs-ing,   nev-er, nev-er, nev-er, nev-er,

C♯m   A   E   B/D♯ C♯m   A A/B

Repeat and Fade

nev-er, nev-er, nev - er be. _
you to make love to me. _
nev-er, nev-er, nev - er be. _

BLUE SKY

Words and Music by
DICKEY BETTS

Walk a - long the riv - er,
Don't fly mister blue bird, I'm just
Good old Sun - day mornin' bells are

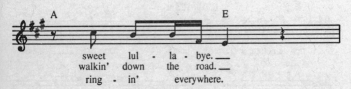

sweet lul - la - bye.
walkin' down the road.
ring - in' everywhere.

They just keep on flow - in'.
Early mornin' sunshine,
Goin' to Carolina, _____

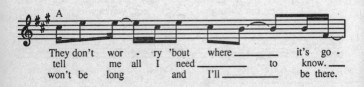

They don't wor - ry 'bout where _____ it's go -
tell me all I need _____ to know. _____
won't be long and I'll _____ be there.

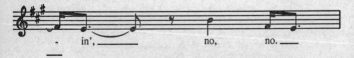

- in', _____ no, no. _____

1. E   B   A

(Instrumental)

2.,3. E   A

B   A   E   A

You're my __ Blue Sky. __ You're my sun - ny day. __

B   A

Lord,   you know   it   makes __ me high __ when ya

E   A

turn   your love __ my   way. __

A   **To Coda** ⊕ F#m

Turn your love   my   way,   yeah. __

E   B   A   **D.C. al Coda**

(Instrumental)

CODA
⊕   A   A(add2)   E

way. __

BORN TO BE WILD

Words and Music by
MARS BONFIRE

41

BUT IT'S ALRIGHT

Words and Music by JEROME L. JACKSON
and PIERRE TUBBS

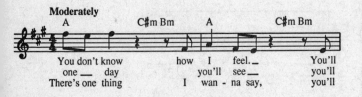

Moderately

You don't know how I feel.__ You'll
one __ day you'll see __ you'll
There's one thing I wan-na say, you'll

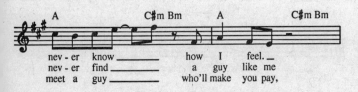

nev - er know _____ how I feel. __
nev - er find _____ a guy like me
meet a guy _____ who'll make you pay,

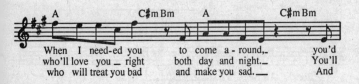

When I need-ed you to come a-round, you'd
who'll love you _ right both day and night. __ You'll
who will treat you bad and make you sad. __ And

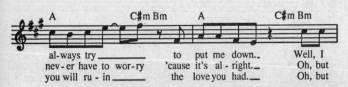

al-ways try to put me down. Well, I
nev-er have to wor-ry 'cause it's al-right. Oh, but
you will ru-in the love you had. __ Oh, but

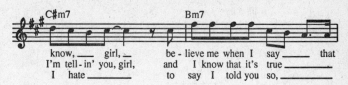

C#m7　　　　　　　Bm7

know, __ girl, __ be - lieve me when I say __ that
I'm tell - in' you, girl, and I know that it's true __
I hate __ to say I told you so, __

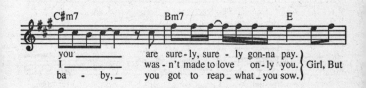

C#m7　　　　　　　Bm7　　　　　　E

you __ are sure - ly, sure - ly gon-na pay. ）
I __ was - n't made to love on - ly you. 〉 Girl, But
ba - by, __ you got to reap _ what _ you sow. ）

To Coda ⊕

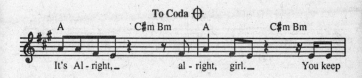

A　　　　C#m Bm　　A　　　　C#m Bm

It's Al - right, __ al - right, girl. __ You keep

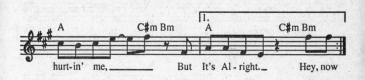

A　　　　C#m Bm　　┌1.⎤ A　　　　C#m Bm

hurt - in' me, __ But It's Al - right. __ Hey, now

┌2.⎤ A　　　　C#m Bm　　A　　　　C#m Bm

It's Al - right, __ oh, yeah. *(Instrumental)*

A　　C#m Bm　　A　　C#m Bm　　A　　C#m Bm

44

Oh, _____ oh, yeah _

my, my, my ba - by, _____ I said _

it's al - right, _ al - right girl. _ Hey, now

D.S. al Coda

it's al - right, al - right, girl. _

CODA

right, girl. _ You are pay-in' now, _ But

It's Al - right. Good-bye, love, good -

Repeat and Fade

bye, girl. _____ You're

BROWN EYED GIRL

Words and Music by
VAN MORRISON

Moderately

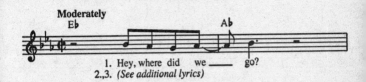

1. Hey, where did we ___ go?
2.,3. *(See additional lyrics)*

Days ___ when the rains ___ came,

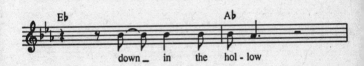

down ___ in the hol - low

play - in' a new ___ game,

laugh-ing and a - run-ning, hey, ___ hey,

skip - ping and a jump - ing.

46

In the mis- ty morn- ing fog __ with

our hearts a-thump- in', and you,

my Brown Eyed Girl. _____

You, my Brown Eyed Girl. __

Do you re-mem- ber when

CHORUS

we used to sing: __ sha la __ la la __

__ la la __ la la __ la la la te da. __

Sha la_ la la_ la la_ la la_

_ la la la te da_ la te da._

Additional Lyrics

2. Whatever happened to Tuesday and so slow
   Going down the old mine with a transistor radio
   Standing in the sunlight laughing
   Hiding behind a rainbow's wall
   Slipping and a-sliding
   All along the waterfall
   With you, my Brown Eyed Girl
   You, my Brown Eyed Girl.
   Do you remember when we used to sing:
   Chorus

3. So hard to find my way, now that I'm all on my own
   I saw you just the other day, my, how you have grown
   Cast my memory back there, Lord
   Sometime I'm overcome thinking 'bout
   Making love in the green grass
   Behind the stadium
   With you, my Brown Eyed Girl
   With you, my Brown Eyed Girl.
   Do you remember when we used to sing:
   Chorus

CARRY ON WAYWARD SON

Words and Music by
KERRY LIVGREN

Moderately

Car-ry on, my way - ward son; there'll be peace when you ___ are done. Lay your wea - ry head ___ to rest; ___ don't you cry no ___ more.

(Instrumental)

Once I rose a - bove the noise and con - fu - sion
Mas-quer - ad - ing as a man with a rea - son,

just to get a glimpse be - yond this il - lu - sion.
my cha - rade is the e - vent of the sea - son.

I was soar - ing ev - er high - er,
And if I claim to be a wise man,

but I flew too ___ high.
it sure - ly means that I don't know.

Though my eyes could see, I still was a blind man.
On a storm - y sea of mov - ing e - mo - tion,

Though my mind could think, I still was a mad - man.
tossed a - bout, I'm like a ship on the o - cean.

I hear the voic - es when I'm dream - ing.
I set a course for winds of for - tune,

I can hear them say:
but I hear the voic - es say:

Car - ry on, my way - ward son; ___

there'll be peace when you __ are done. __

Lay your wea - ry head __ to rest; _____

don't you cry no __ more. *(Instrumental)*

Car - ry on; you will al - ways re - mem - ber. __

Car - ry on; noth - ing e - quals the splen - dor.

Now your life's no long - er emp - ty; __

sure - ly heav - en waits for you.

CRAZY LITTLE THING
CALLED LOVE

Words and Music by
FREDDIE MERCURY

This thing _ called love _ I just _ can't han-dle it, _ this thing _ called love _ I must _ get round to it, I ain't read-y. Cra-zy Lit-tle Thing Called Love, _ this thing _ (This thing) called love _ _ (called love) it cries _ (like a ba-by) in a

53

COCAINE

Words and Music by
JOHN J. CALE

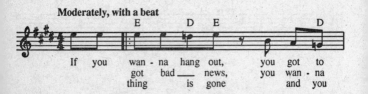

If you wan-na hang out, you got to
got bad news, you wan-na
thing is gone and you

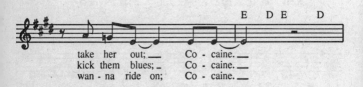

take her out; ___ Co - caine. ___
kick them blues; ___ Co - caine. ___
wan-na ride on; Co - caine. ___

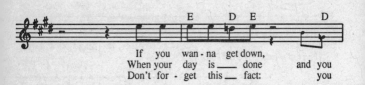

If you wan-na get down,
When your day is ___ done and you
Don't for-get this ___ fact: you

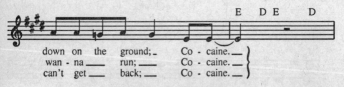

down on the ground; ___ Co - caine. ___
wan-na ___ run; ___ Co - caine. ___
can't get ___ back; ___ Co - caine. ___

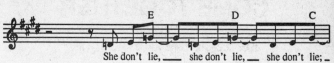

She don't lie, ___ she don't lie, ___ she don't lie; ___

___ Co - caine. ___

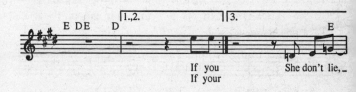

If you
If your

She don't lie, ___

___ she don't lie, ___ she don't lie; ___

___ Co - caine. ___

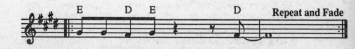

Repeat and Fade

COME TOGETHER

Words and Music by
JOHN LENNON and PAUL McCARTNEY

Moderately slow, with a double time feeling

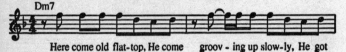

Here come old flat-top, He come   groov-ing up slow-ly, He got

Joo   Joo eye-ball, He one   ho - ly roll-er, He got

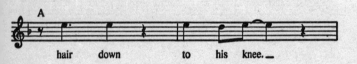

hair   down   to   his   knee.

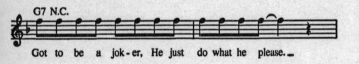

Got   to   be   a   jok-er,   He just   do what he   please.

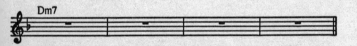

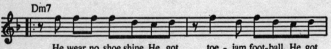

He wear no shoe shine, He got   toe - jam foot-ball, He got
He Bag Pro-duc-tion, He got   wal - rus gum-boot, He got
He roll-er coast-er, He got   ear - ly warn-ing, He got

57

DA YA THINK I'M SEXY

Words and Music by ROD STEWART
CARMINE APPICE and DUANE HITCHINGS

Medium Disco beat

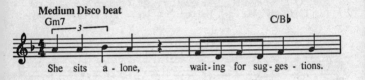

She sits a-lone, wait-ing for sug-ges-tions.

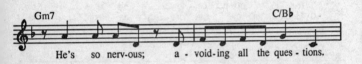

He's so nerv-ous; a-void-ing all the ques-tions.

His lips are dry Her heart is gent-ly pound-ing.

Don't you just know ex-act-ly what they're think-ing? __ If __

__ you want my bod-y and __ you think I'm sex-y, come __

__ on, sug-ar, let me know. __ If __ you real-ly need me, just __

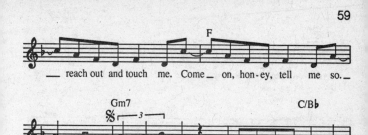

— reach out and touch me. Come — on, hon - ey, tell me so. —

— He's act - ing shy, look - ing for an an - swer.
They wake at dawn, 'cause all the birds are sing - ing.

"Come on,— hon - ey, let's spend the night to - geth - er." "Now,
Two to - tal stran-gers. But that ain't what they're think-ing!

hold on — a min - ute be - fore we go much fur - ther.
Out - side — it's cold; mist - y and it's rain - ing.

Give me a dime, so I can phone my moth - er."
They got each oth - er. Nei - ther one's com-plain - ing.

They catch a cab — to his high - rise a - part - ment. At
He says, "I'm sor - ry, but I'm out of milk and cof - fee."

last — he can tell her ex - act - ly what his heart meant. } If —
"Nev - er mind,— sug - ar. We can watch the ear - ly mov - ie."

60

DON'T STAND SO CLOSE TO ME

Words and Music by
STING

62

Don't Stand So

Close To Me,

Don't Stand So Close To Me.

Her friends are
(Instrumental)

so jeal-ous. You know how bad girls — get.

Some-times it's not so ea-sy to be the

teach-er's — pet. Temp-ta-tion, frus-tra-tion,

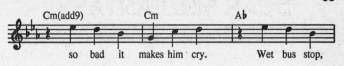

so bad it makes him cry. Wet bus stop,

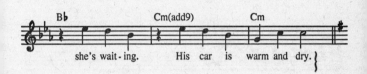

she's wait-ing. His car is warm and dry.

Don't Stand So ____ Close To Me.__

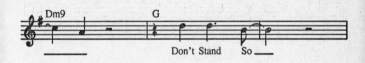

____ Don't Stand So ____

Close To Me. ____

CODA

Don't Stand So ____ (don't stand so)

Close To Me. ____

DEAR MR. FANTASY

Words and Music by JAMES CAPALDI,
CHRIS WOOD and STEVE WINWOOD

Moderately slow, with a beat

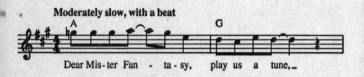

Dear Mis- ter Fan - ta - sy, play us a tune,

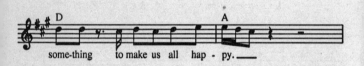

some-thing to make us all hap - py.

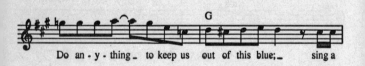

Do an - y - thing to keep us out of this blue; sing a

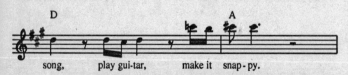

song, play gui-tar, make it snap - py.

You are the one _ who can make us all glad _ but

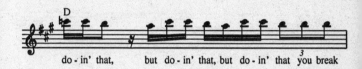

do - in' that, but do - in' that, but do - in' that you break

down in tears. Please don't be sad _ if it was a

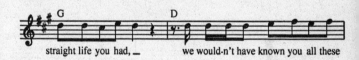

straight life you had, _ we would-n't have known you all these

years.

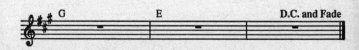

DON'T STOP

Words and Music by
CHRISTINE McVIE

Moderate Rock shuffle

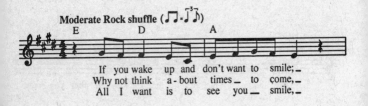

If you wake up and don't want to smile;
Why not think a - bout times to come,
All I want is to see you smile,

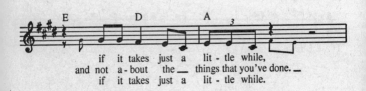

if it takes just a lit - tle while,
and not a - bout the things that you've done.
if it takes just a lit - tle while.

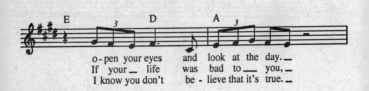

o - pen your eyes and look at the day.
If your life was bad to you,
I know you don't be - lieve that it's true.

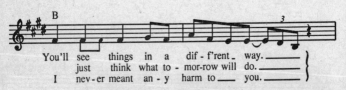

You'll see things in a dif - f'rent way.
just think what to - mor-row will do.
I nev - er meant an - y harm to you.

67

Don't   Stop   think-ing a-bout to - mor - row.

Don't   Stop,   it - 'll soon _ be   here. ___

It - 'll be _____   bet-ter than be - fore._

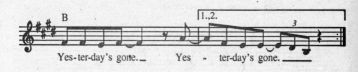

Yes-ter-day's gone._   Yes - ter-day's gone. ___

- ter-day's gone. ___   Ooh, ___

Repeat and Fade

___   don't you look _ back.

DOO DOO DOO DOO DOO
(HEARTBREAKER)

**Words and Music by MICK JAGGER
and KEITH RICHARDS**

Moderate Rock

The po - lice in New York Cit-y, ___

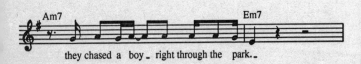

they chased a boy ___ right through the park. ___

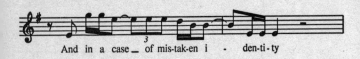

And in a case ___ of mis-tak-en i - den-ti-ty

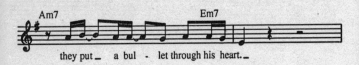

they put ___ a bul - let through his heart. ___

Heart - break - er ___ with your for - ty-four,

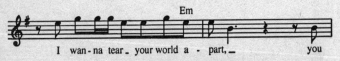

I wan-na tear ___ your world a - part, ___ you

heart break-er ___ with your for-ty-four,___

I wan-na tear ___ your world a - part. ___

A ten-year-old girl on a street cor-ner,

Stick-ing nee - dles in her arm. ___ She

died ___ in the dirt of an al-ley-way, ___

her moth-er said ___ she had ___ no chance, ___ no chance!

Heart break-er, ___ heart break-er, ___

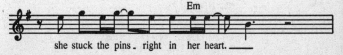

she stuck the pins ___ right in her heart. ___

70

DREAMS

Words and Music by
STEVIE NICKS

DREAM ON

Words and Music by
STEVEN TYLER

Moderately slow

Ev-'ry time _ that I look in the mir - ror,

all these lines on my face get-tin' clear - er.

The past _ is gone; _ it went by like _

_ dusk to dawn. _ Is-n't that the way _

ev-'ry-bod-y's got _ their dues _____ in life _ to pay? _

I know no-bod - y knows

where _ it comes and where _ it goes. _

may-be to-mor-row the good Lord will take you a-way.

Dream On, ___ Dream On, ___

Dream On, ___ dream your-self a dream come

true. ___ Dream On, ___ Dream On, ___

Dream On ___ and dream un-til your dream comes

true. Dream On, ___ Dream On, ___

Dream On, ___ Dream On, ___ Dream On, ___ Dream On, ___

Dream On, __ ah. Ah. ____

Sing with me, sing for the years, __

sing for the laugh-ter 'n' sing ____ for the tears. ____

Sing with me if it's just for to-day, __

1. may-be to-mor-row the good Lord will take you a-way.

2. may-be to-mor-row the good Lord __ will take you a-

way.

Repeat and Fade

DUST IN THE WIND

Words and Music by
KERRY LIVGREN

EMOTIONAL RESCUE

**Words and Music by MICK JAGGER
and KEITH RICHARDS**

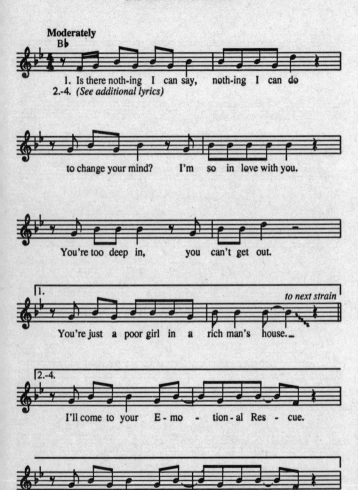

Moderately

Bb

1. Is there noth-ing I can say, noth-ing I can do
2.-4. *(See additional lyrics)*

to change your mind? I'm so in love with you.

You're too deep in, you can't get out.

[1.]

to next strain

You're just a poor girl in a rich man's house.

[2.-4.]

I'll come to your E - mo - tion - al Res - cue.

I'll come to your E - mo - tion - al Res - cue.

82

mine, ___   mine, ___   Ooh!

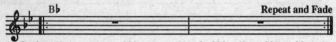

Spoken: Um, yes, you could be mine. . . Vocal ad lib. - (See additional lyrics)

Additional Lyrics

Verse 2: Don't you know promises were never made to keep?
            Just like the night, they dissolve in sleep.
            I'll be your saviour, steadfast and true. *(To 2nd ending:)*

Bridge: 2. Yeah, I'm crying baby.
              I'm like a child, baby.
         3. Like a child, yeah.
              So like a child, like a child, like a child, like a child.

Verse 3: You think you're one of a special breed,
            You think that you're his pet Pekinese.
            I'll be your saviour, steadfast and true. *(To 3rd ending:)*

Bridge: 4. Last night I was dreaming.
         5. How you'd be mine, but I was crying
         6. Like a child. Yeah, I was crying,
         7. Crying like a child. You will be
              Mine, mine, mine, mine, mine,
         8. All mine. You could be mine, could be mine,
              Be mine, all mine.

Verse 4: I come to you, so silent in the night,
            So stealthy, so animal quiet.
            I'll be your saviour, steadfast and true. *(To 4th ending:)*

Vocal
ad lib.: *. . . tonight and every night. I will be your knight in shining armour*
           Coming to your Emotional Rescue.
           You will be mine, you will be mine, all mine.
           You will be mine, you will be mine, all mine.
           I want to be your knight in shining armour, riding across the
           Desert with a fine Arab charger.
           (Instr. ad lib. . . Fade)

FOREVER MAN

Words and Music by
JERRY LYNN WILLIAMS

Moderately fast

How man-y times __ must I __ tell __ you, ba - by,
(Instrumental)

how man-y bridg - es I've __ got to __ cross? __

How man-y times __ must __ I ex - plain __ my - self

'fore I can talk __ to the boss, __

'fore __ I can talk __ to __ the boss? __

(Instrumental)

How man-y times __ must I __ say __ I love __ you __
How man-y times __ must I __ say __ I love __ you __

84

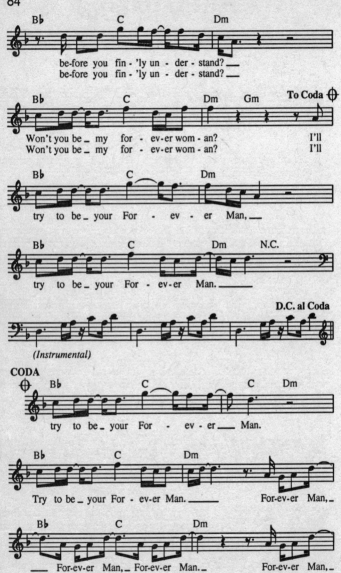

FLY LIKE AN EAGLE

Words and Music by
STEVE MILLER

till I'm free, _____ right _____

through the rev - o - lu - tion. _____

_____ Feed the ba - bies who

don't have e - nough _ to eat. Shoe the chil -

- dren with no shoes on _ their feet.

House the peo - ple liv - in' in _ the street.

Oh, _____ there's a so - lu -

- tion. Doo doot - n doo doot.

[1.,2.,3.] [4.]
D.S. and Fade

Doo doot - n doo doot.

FREE BIRD

Words and Music by ALLEN COLLINS
and RONNIE VAN ZANT

Moderately

If I leave here to-mor-row,
Bye, bye ba-by it's been a sweet love

Would you still re-mem-ber me?
though this feel-ing I can't change.

For I must be trav-'ling on now
But please don't take it so bad-ly

'cause there's too man-y plac-es I've got to see.
'cause the Lord knows I'm to blame.

But if I stayed here with

you, girl, things just could-n't be the same.

'Cause I'm as free __ as a bird now,

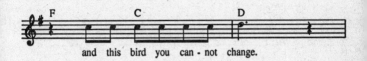

and this bird you can-not change.

And this bird you can-not change. __

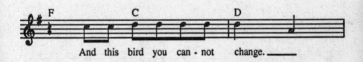

And this bird you can-not change. __

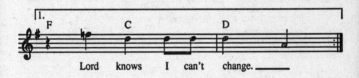

Lord knows I can't change. __

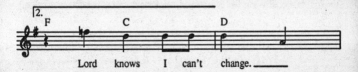

Lord knows I can't change. __

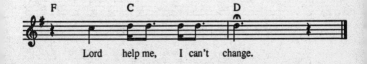

Lord help me, I can't change.

FREE RIDE

Words and Music by
DAN HARTMAN

Rock 'n' Roll

The moun-tain is high___ the val-ley is low___ and

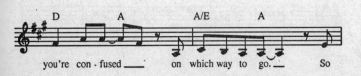

you're con-fused___ on which way to go.___ So

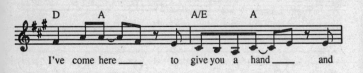

I've come here___ to give you a hand___ and

lead us in-to the pro-mised land.___ So,

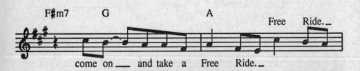

come on___ and take a Free Ride.___

Come on ___ and sit here by my side. ___

Come on ___ and take a Free Ride.

(Instrumental)

All

o - ver the coun - try I've seen it the same. ___

No - bod - y's win - ning at this kind of game. ___ We've

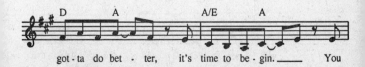

got - ta do bet - ter, it's time to be - gin. ___ You

know all the an - swers must come from with - in. ___ So

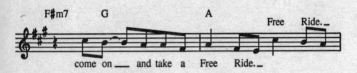

F#m7 G A Free Ride. ___

come on ___ and take a Free Ride. ___

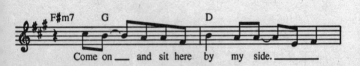

F#m7 G D

Come on ___ and sit here by my side. ___

F#m7 G D

Come on ___ and take a Free Ride.

(Instrumental)

A

Yeh yeh yeh yeh

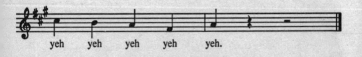

yeh yeh yeh yeh yeh.

GIMME THREE STEPS

Words and Music by ALLEN COLLINS
and RONNIE VAN ZANT

Moderately

1. I was cut - ting the rug____ down at a
3. (See additional lyrics)

place called the Jug____ with a girl named Lin - da Lu,

____ When____ in walked a man____ with a

gun in his hand____ and he was look - ing for you know who.____

____ He said, "Hey____ there fel - low with the

hair col - ored yel - low, what you try - in' to prove____

____ 'Cause that's my wo - man there____ and I'm a

man who _ cares _ and this might be all _ for you _

A7

To Chorus
2nd time only

D

2. I was
Oh won't you

scared and fear - ing for my life _ I was

A7

shak - in' like a leaf on a tree _ 'Cause he was

D

lean, mean, big and bad, _ Lord,

E7   A7

point - in' that gun at me _ Oh,

D

wait a min - ute mis - ter I did - n't e - ven kiss her,

G   E7

don't want no trou - ble with you _ And I know _

D

_ you don't owe me but I wish you'd _ let _ me

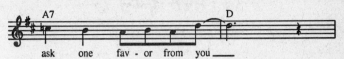

ask   one   fav - or   from   you ___

Chorus

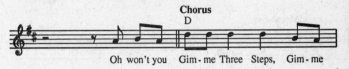

Oh won't you Gim - me Three Steps, Gim - me

Three Steps mis - ter, Gim - me Three Steps to - ward the door ___

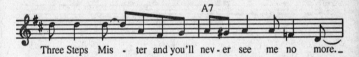

___   Gim - me Three   Steps,   Gim - me

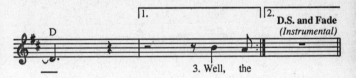

Three Steps Mis - ter and you'll nev - er see   me no   more. ___

1.

2. **D.S. and Fade**
(Instrumental)

3. Well,   the

Additional Lyrics

3. Well, the crowd cleared away, and I began to pray
   and the water fell on the floor.
   And I'm telling you son, it ain't no fun staring
   straight down a forty four
   Well, he turned and screamed at Linda Lu
   and that's the break I was looking for.
   And you could hear me screaming a mile away
   As I headed out toward the door.

   Chorus

FUNK #49

**Words and Music by JOE WALSH,
DALE PETERS and JIM FOX**

(Instrumental)

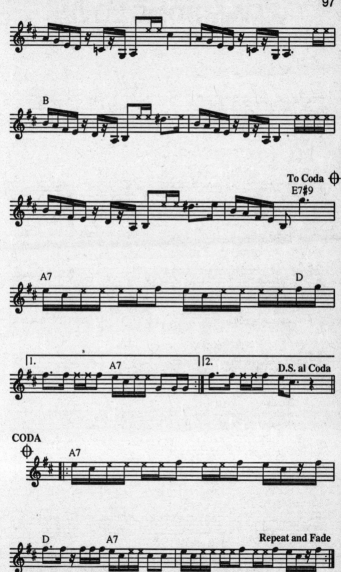

GIMME SOME LOVIN'

Words and Music by SPENCER DAVIS,
MUFF WINWOOD and STEVE WINWOOD

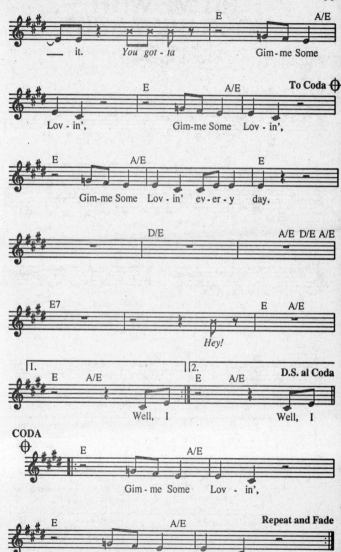

HIT ME WITH YOUR BEST SHOT

Words and Music by
EDDIE SCHWARTZ

I CAN SEE FOR MILES

Words and Music by
PETER TOWNSHEND

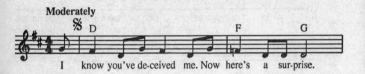

I know you've de-ceived me. Now here's a sur-prise.

I know that you have 'cos there's

ma- gic in ___ my eyes ___

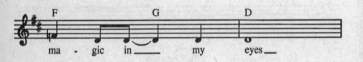

I Can See For Miles and

miles and miles and miles and

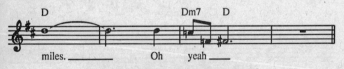

miles. ___ Oh yeah ___

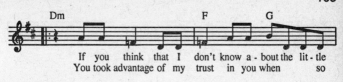
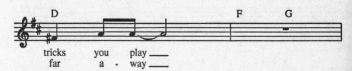
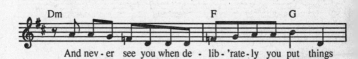
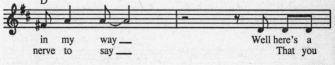
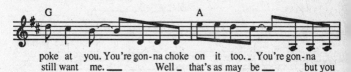

104

I LOVE ROCK 'N' ROLL

Words and Music by ALAN MERRILL
and JAKE HOOKER

I saw him danc-ing there by the re-cord ma-chine. I knew he must have been a-bout sev-en-teen. The beat was go-ing strong, play-ing my fav'rite song, and I could tell it would-n't be long on, till he was with me, yeah,

smiled, so I got up and asked for his name. "That don't mat-ter," he said, "cause it's all the same." I said, "Can I take you home where we can be a-lone?" And next, we were mov-ing on, and he was with me, yeah,

I SHOT THE SHERIFF

Words and Music by
BOB MARLEY

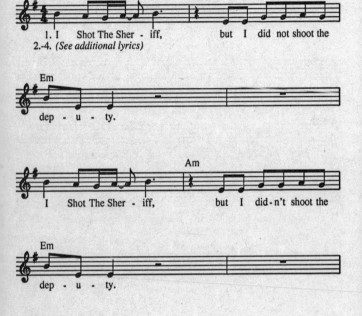

Moderately Slow, with a beat

1. I Shot The Sheriff, but I did not shoot the

2.-4. *(See additional lyrics)*

dep - u - ty.

I Shot The Sheriff, but I did-n't shoot the

dep - u - ty.

All a-round in my home town, they're

try - ing to track me down. They

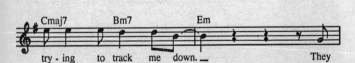

say they want to bring me in guilt - y   for the

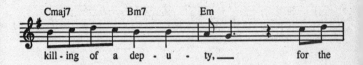

kill - ing of a dep - u - ty, ___   for the

life of a dep - u - ty. ___   But I say: ___

(Instrumental)

Additional Lyrics

2. I Shot The Sheriff, but I swear it was in self-defense.
   I Shot The Sheriff, and they say it is a capital offense.
   Sheriff John Brown always hated me; for what, I don't know.
   Every time that I plant a seed, he said, "Kill it before it grows."
   He said, "Kill it before it grows." But I say:

3. I Shot The Sheriff, but I swear it was in self-defense.
   I Shot The Sheriff, but I swear it was in self-defense.
   Freedom came my way one day, and I started out of town.
   All of a sudden, I see Sheriff John Brown aiming to shoot me down.
   So I shot, I shot him down. But I say:

4. I Shot The Sheriff, but I did not shoot the deputy.
   I Shot The Sheriff, but I didn't shoot the deputy.
   Reflexes got the better of me, and what is to be must be.
   Every day, the bucket goes to the well, but one day the bottom will drop out.
   Yes, one day the bottom will drop out. But I say:

I'M A MAN

Words and Music by STEVE WINWOOD
and JIMMY MILLER

Well, my pad is ver - y mes - sy, got the
got to keep my im - age while sus -

whis - kers on my chin.
pend - ed on a throne that looks

Nev - er had no prob - lems 'cause I
out up - on a king - dom filled with

al - ways pay the rent. I've
peo - ple all un - known, who im -

got no time for lov - in' 'cause my
ag - ine I'm not hu - man and my

time is all used up; I
heart is made of stone, and I

lat - ing to each oth - er just how

strong the will can be in re -

sist - ing all in - volv - ment with each

groov - y chick we see. I'm A Man, yes, I

am, but I can't help but love you so. I'm A

Man, yes, I am, but I can't help but love you so.

D.S. al Coda

CODA

So, I've

(Instrumental)

Rubato (slowly)

IT'S ONLY ROCK 'N' ROLL
(BUT I LIKE IT)

Words and Music by MICK JAGGER
and KEITH RICHARDS

cheat-ing heart ___ if ___ I broke down and cried? __
it slide on by ya, would _ ya think the boy's in - sane? __

A G E

__ If I cried? _____ }
__ He's in - sane. _____ } I said

A

I know _ It's On - ly Rock 'N' Roll but I

E   A

like it. _____   I know _ It's

E D

On - ly Rock 'N' Roll but I like it, like it,

A E A

yes, I do. _ Oh, well, I like it,   I

E A

like it,   I like it.   I said

D A D A

can't you see _ that this old boy _ has been - a

JESUS IS JUST ALRIGHT

by ARTHUR REYNOLDS

Do do do do __ do do __ do do. __

Do do do do __ do do __ do do. __

Do do do do __ do do. __

oh yeah. __

Moderate Waltz

(Instrumental)

Je - sus, _____

He's my

friend. ____
(Instrumental)

LADY MADONNA

Words and Music by
JOHN LENNON and PAUL McCARTNEY

Brightly, with a beat

(Instrumental)

La - dy Ma-don - na,   chil - dren at your feet,___
La - dy Ma-don - na,   ba - by at your breast,___
La - dy Ma-don - na,   ly - ing on the bed,___
La - dy Ma-don - na,   chil - dren at your feet,___

Won - der how you man - age to make___
Won - ders how you man - age to feed___
Lis - ten to the mu - sic play - ing___
Won - der how you man - age to make___

To Coda

___ ends meet.___   Who finds the mon -
___ the rest.___   (Instrumental ad lib.)
___ in your head.___   (Instrumental ad lib.)
___ ends meet.___

- ey   when you pay the rent,___

Did you think that mon-ey was heav-en sent?

Fri - day night ar - rives with-out a suit - case,
3. Tues-day af - ter-noon is nev - er end - ing,

Sun - day morn - ing creep-ing like a
Wednes-day morn - ing pa - pers did - n't

nun, Mon-day's child has learned to tie his
come, Thurs-day night your stock-ings need - ed

boot - lace,
mend - ing. } See

how they run!

CODA

(Instrumental)

LAY DOWN SALLY

Words and Music by ERIC CLAPTON,
MARCY LEVY and GEORGE TERRY

Bright Beat

LAYLA

**Words and Music by ERIC CLAPTON
and JIM GORDON**

LET IT RIDE

Words and Music by RANDY BACHMAN
and CHARLES TURNER

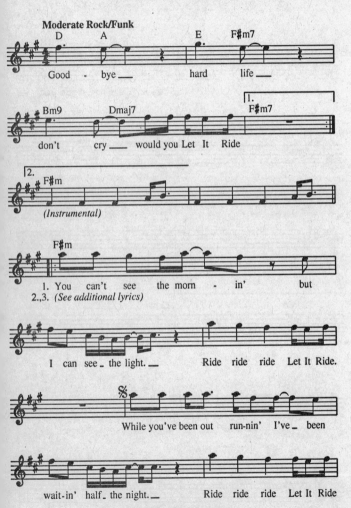

Moderate Rock/Funk

Good - bye __ hard life __

don't cry __ would you Let It Ride

1.

2. (Instrumental)

1. You can't see the morn - in' but
2.,3. *(See additional lyrics)*

I can see __ the light. __ Ride ride ride Let It Ride.

While you've been out run-nin' I've __ been

wait-in' half the night. __ Ride ride ride Let It Ride

Additional Lyrics

2. Babe, my life is not complete
   I never see you smile
   Ride ride ride let it ride
   Baby you want for forgivin' time
   And that's just not my style
   Ride ride ride let it ride
   And would you cry -- etc. --

3. I've been doin' things worthwhile
   And you've been bookin' time
   Ride ride ride let it ride
   And would you cry -- etc. --

LICK IT UP

**Words and Music by PAUL STANLEY
and VINCENT CUSANO**

Don't wan-na wait 'til you know me bet-ter.
Don't need to wait for an in-vi-ta-tion;

Let's just be glad for the
you got-ta live like you're

time to-geth-er.
on va-ca-tion.

Life's such a treat and it's time you taste it.
There's some-thin' sweet you can't buy for mon-ey.

There ain't a rea-son on
It's all you need, so be-

earth to waste it. }
lieve me, ho-ney. }

It ain't a crime to be

good to your-self. Lick It Up, Lick

THE LOCO-MOTION

Words and Music by
GERRY GOFFIN and CAROLE KING

Moderately

Ev-'ry-bod-y's do - in' a brand new dance now. C'm on, ba - by do ___ The Lo - co - mo - tion. I know you'll get to like it if you give it a chance ___ now. C'm on, ba - by do ___ The Lo - co - mo - tion. My lit - tle ba - by sis - ter can do it with ease, ___ It's eas - i - er than learn - in' your A B C's, ___ So come on, come on, do ___ The Lo - co - mo - tion with

Eb

me.　　You got-ta swing your hips now.

Ab　　　　　　　　　　**Eb**

Come on, ba-by, jump up,＿ jump back.＿

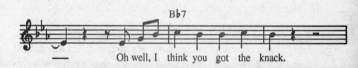

Bb7

＿　　Oh well, I think you got the knack.

Eb　　　　　　　　　　**Cm**

Now that you can do＿ it let's make a chain＿ now.

Eb　　　　　　　　　**Cm**

C'm on, ba-by do＿ The Lo-co-mo-tion.

A

Eb　　　　　　　　　**Cm**

chug-a-chug-a mo-tion like a rail - road train＿ now.

Eb　　　　　　　　**Cm**

C'm on, ba-by do＿ The Lo-co-mo-tion.

Do it nice and eas - y now,_ don't lose con - trol._ A

lit - tle bit of rhy - thm and a lot of soul._

Come on, come on do ____ The Lo - co - mo - tion with

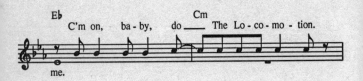

C'm on, baby, do ____ The Lo - co - mo - tion.

me.

Move a - round the floor _ in a lo - co - mo - tion.

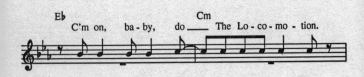

C'm on, baby, do ____ The Lo - co - mo - tion.

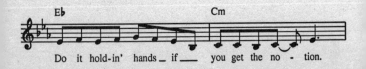

Do it hold - in' hands _ if ____ you get the no - tion.

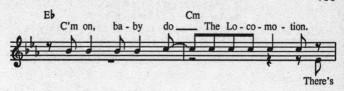

Eb / Cm
C'm on, baby do___ The Lo-co-mo-tion. There's

Ab / Fm
nev-er been a dance_that's so eas-y to do.___ It

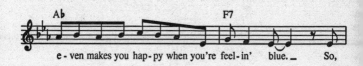

Ab / F7
e-ven makes you hap-py when you're feel-in' blue.___ So,

Eb / Bb9
Come on, come on, do_____ The Lo-co-mo-tion with

Eb / Cm
C'm on, baby do___ The Lo-co-mo-tion.
me.

Eb / Cm
C'm on, baby do___ The Lo-co-mo-tion.

Eb / Cm / Fade
C'm on, baby do___ The Lo-co-mo-tion.

LOW RIDER

Words and Music by SYLVESTER ALLEN, HAROLD R. BROWN,
MORRIS DICKERSON, JERRY GOLDSTEIN, LEROY JORDAN,
LEE OSKAR, CHARLES W. MILLER and HOWARD SCOTT

MAGGIE MAY

Words and Music by ROD STEWART
and MARTIN QUITTENTON

Medium Rock beat

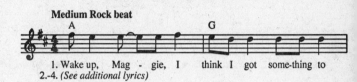

1. Wake up, Mag - gie, I think I got some-thing to
2.-4. *(See additional lyrics)*

say to you. __ It's

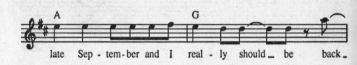

late Sep - tem - ber and I real - ly should __ be back __

__ at __ school. __ I

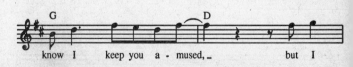

know I keep you a - mused, __ but I

136

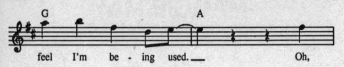

feel I'm be - ing used. ___ Oh,

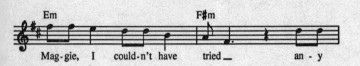

Mag - gie, I could - n't have tried ___ an - y

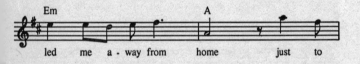

more. _____ You

led me a - way from home just to

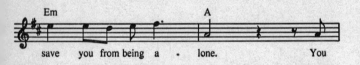

save you from being a - lone. You

stole my heart, ___ and that's ___ what real - ly hurts. ___

___ 2. The

D   Em7

(Instrumental)

G   D   **Repeat and Fade**

Additional Lyrics

2. The morning sun, when it's in your face,
   Really shows your age.
   But that don't worry me none.
   In my eyes, you're everything.
   I laughed at all of your jokes.
   My love you didn't need to coax.
   Oh, Maggie, I couldn't have tried any more.
   You led me away from home
   Just to save you from being alone.
   You stole my soul, and that's a pain I can do without.

3. All I needed was a friend
   To lend a guiding hand.
   But you turned into a lover, and, mother, what a lover!
   You wore me out.
   All you did was wreck my bed,
   And, in the morning, kick me in the head.
   Oh, Maggie, I couldn't have tried any more.
   You led me away from home
   'Cause you didn't want to be alone.
   You stole my heart. I couldn't leave you if I tried.

4. I suppose I could collect my books
   And get on back to school.
   Or steal my daddy's cue
   And make a living out of playing pool.
   Or find myself a rock 'n' roll band
   That needs a helping hand.
   Oh, Maggie, I wish I'd never seen your face.
   You made a first-class fool out of me.
   But I'm as blind as a fool can be.
   You stole my heart, but I love you anyway.

MAGIC CARPET RIDE

Words and Music by JOHN KAY
and RUSHTON MOREVE

| D | C | G | | D | C | G |

You don't know what, we can see, ___

| D | | C | | G | | |

Why don't you tell your dreams to me,

| D | | C | | G | | |

Fan - ta - sy will set you free,

| G | | | | Bb | | |

Close your eyes girl, Look in - side girl,

| C | | | Am7sus | | D9sus | |

Let the sound take you a - way. ___

| D | C | G | | D | C | G |

(Spoken: patter style)
Last night I owned Aladdin's Lamp and so I wished that I could stay.

| D | C | G | | D | C | G |

Before the thing could answer someone came and took the lamp away.

D.S. and Fade

| D | C | G | | D | C | G |

I looked around a lousy candle is all I found. Well

MISSISSIPPI QUEEN

Words and Music by LESLIE WEST, FELIX PAPPALARDI,
CORKY LAING and D. REA

Half-Time Feel

Mis-sis-sip-pi Queen, ___ do you know ___

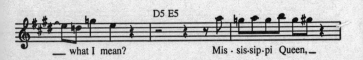

___ what I mean? Mis-sis-sip-pi Queen, ___

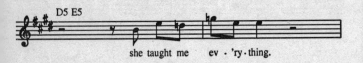

she taught me ev-'ry-thing.

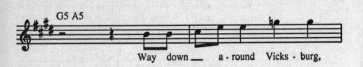

Way down ___ a-round Vicks-burg,

a-round Lou-i-si-an-a way, ___

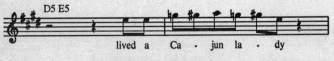

lived a Ca-jun la-dy

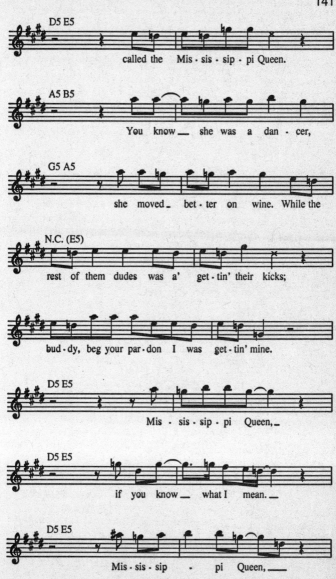

142

| D5 E5 | she taught me | ev - ry - thing. |

| G5 A5 | This la - dy she __ asked me |

| G5 A5 | if I would be her man. ___ |

| D5 E5 | You know __ that I told her |

| D5 E5 | I'd __ do __ what I can |

| A5 B5 | to keep __ her look - in' pret - ty. |

| G5 A5 | Buy her dress - es that shine. __ While the |

N.C. (E5)

rest of them dudes was a' mak - in' their bread;

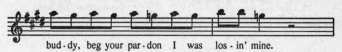

bud-dy, beg your par-don I was los-in' mine.

You know __ she was a danc-er, __

she moved __ bet-ter on wine. While the

rest of them dudes __ was get-tin' their kicks;

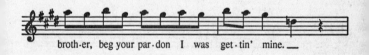

broth-er, beg your par-don I was get-tin' mine. __

Hey, _____ Mis-sis-sip-pi Queen. __

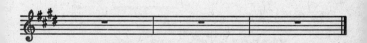

MORE THAN A FEELING

Words and Music by
TOM SCHOLZ

Moderate Rock Tempo

1. I woke up this morn - ing and the sun was gone,— the
2. So man - y peo - ple have come and gone,—— the
3. *(See additional lyrics)*

turned on some mu - sic to start my day— I
fac - es fade— as the years— go by;— yet

lost my - self— in a fam - il - iar song.—— I
I still re - call as I wan - der on,— as

closed my eyes— and I slipped a - way.——
clear as the sun— in the sum - mer sky.——

(Instrumental)

It's

(More Than A Feel - ing)—

More Than A Feel - ing,

When I

hear that old song _ they used to play. _

I be - gin dream - ing 'til I

To Coda II

see Mar - i - anne _ walk a - way,

I see my Mar - i - anne walk-in' a - way. _

1.

(Instrumental)

2.

(Instrumental)

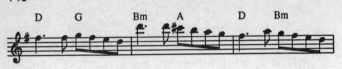

D.S. al Coda I

CODA I

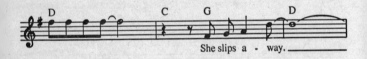

slips a - way.___ *(Instrumental)*

She slips a - way._____

D.S.S. al Coda II

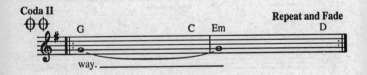

Coda II

Repeat and Fade

way._____

Additional Lyrics

3. When I'm tired and thinking cold
   I hide in my music, forget the day
   And dream of a girl I used to know
   I closed my eyes and she slipped away.

THE NIGHT THEY DROVE OLD DIXIE DOWN

Words and Music by
ROBBIE ROBERTSON

Moderately

1. Vir - gil Caine _ is the name, _ and I served _

_ on the Dan - ville train, _

'Til Stone - man's Cav - al - ry came _ and

tore up the tracks a - gain. _

In the win - ter of six - ty five, we were

hun - gry, just bare - ly a - live. _

148

By May the tenth, Rich-mond had fell; _ it's a time _

_ I re-mem-ber, oh, _ so well.

Chorus

The Night They Drove _

_ Old Dix - ie Down, _ And the

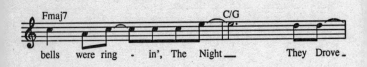

bells were ring - in', The Night _ They Drove _

_ Old Dix - ie Down. _ And the

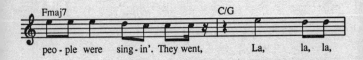

peo - ple were sing - in'. They went, La, la, la,

la,   la,   la,   La, la,   la,   la,   la,   la, _

   la,   la, _____ *(Instrumental)*

(Instrumental)

The

Additional Lyrics

2. Back with my wife in Tennessee
   When one day she called to me
   "Virgil, quick, come see:
   There goes Robert E. Lee!"
   Now, I don't mind choppin' wood
   And I don't care if the money's no good,
   Ya take what ya need and ya leave the rest
   But they should never have taken
   The very best.
   (Chorus)

3. Like my father before me
   I will work the land.
   And like my brother above me
   Who took a rebel stand.
   He was just eighteen, proud and brave,
   But a Yankee laid him in his grave.
   I swear by the mud below my feet,
   You can't raise a Caine back up
   When he's in defeat.
   (Chorus)

MY GENERATION

Words and Music by
PETER TOWNSHEND

Moderately

Peo-ple try to put us down ___ (talk-in' 'bout My

Gen - er - a - tion) Just be-cause we get a - round ___

(talk - in' 'bout My Gen - er - a - tion) Things they do look

aw - ful cold ___ (talk-in' 'bout My Gen - er - a - tion)

Hope I die be - fore ___ I get old (talk - in' 'bout My Gen-

This is My Gen - er - a - tion ___ - er - a - tion)

This is My Gen-er - a - tion ba - by ___

OH! DARLING

Words and Music by
JOHN LENNON and PAUL McCARTNEY

Oh — Dar - ling, — please be - lieve me, —
Dar - ling, — if you leave me, —

I'll nev - er do you — no harm; — Be-
I'll nev - er make it — a - lone; — Be-

lieve me when I tell you, I'll nev - er do you — no
lieve me when I beg you, Don't ev - er leave me — a-

harm. — Oh, — lone. —

When you told me — you did-n't

need me an-y-more.. Well you know I near-ly broke down— and

cried _____ When you told me ___ you did-n't

need me an-y-more, ___ Well you know, I near-ly fell down and

died. _____ Oh, { Dar - ling, ___ if you
                   { Dar - ling, ___ please be-

leave me, ___ I'll nev - er make it ___ a-
lieve me, ___ I'll nev - er let _____ you

lone; _____ (Spoken) Oh, Be - lieve me when I tell you
down. ___ *believe me darling* Be - lieve me when I tell you

I'll nev - er do you ___ no harm. _____

(Spoken)
Believe me, darling When you I'll nev - er do you ___ no

harm.
(Instrumental)

RAMBLIN' MAN

Words and Music by
DICKEY BETTS

Moderately fast

Lord, I ___ was born ___ a Ram - blin'

Man, _____ try'n' to make a liv - in' and

do - in' the best I _____. can. ___

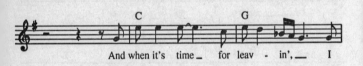

And when it's time ___ for leav - in', ___ I

hope you'll un - der - stand _____

that I was born ___ a Ram - blin'

Man.   Well, my   fa - ther was __   a gam -
                         on   my way __   to New __

__ bler   down   in   Geor - gia, __
__   Or - leans   this   morn : in', __

and he   wound   up   on __ the wrong __
      leav - in'   out __   of Nash -

__ end   of   a   gun. _____   And
- ville, Ten - nes - see. _____   They're

I   was   born __   in   the   back __   seat __   of   a
al - ways   hav - in'   a   good time   down __ on the

Grey - hound __   bus _____
bay - ou,   Lord, _____   them

roll - in' __ down   High - way   For - ty - one. __
del - ta wom - en   think   the   world   of   me. __

_____   Lord,   I   was   born __

a Ram - blin' Man,

try'n' to make a liv - in' and do - in' the best I

can. And when it's time for

leav - in' I hope you'll un - der - stand

that I was born

1. a Ram - blin' Man. I'm

2. Man. Lord, I was born

Repeat and Fade

a Ram - blin' Man.

REBEL, REBEL

Words and Music by
DAVID BOWIE

With a heavy beat

Do do do do __ do do do do

Got your moth-er   in a   whirl, __
Got your moth-er   in a   whirl, __ 'cause she's

she's not   sure if you're a   boy or a   girl. __
not   sure if you're a   boy or a   girl. __

Hey   babe, __   your hair's al - right. __
Hey   babe, __   your hair's al - right. __

Hey, babe,   let's go out to - night. __ }
Hey, babe,   let's stay out to - night. __ }

You like   me and I   like it   all, __

we like danc-ing and we   look di - vine. __

158

You love bands when they play it hard, —

you want more and you want it fast —

Put you down and say I'm wrong, —

you tack - y thing, and put them on. —

Reb - el, Reb - el you've torn your dress, —

Reb - el, Reb - el your face is a mess. —

Reb - el, Reb - el how could they know —

hot tramp, I love you so. —

REELIN' IN THE YEARS

Words and Music by WALTER BECKER
and DONALD FAGEN

Moderately

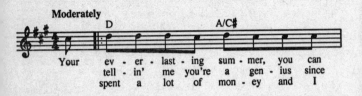

Your ev- er- last- ing sum- mer, you can
tell- in' me you're a gen- ius since
spent a lot of mon- ey and I

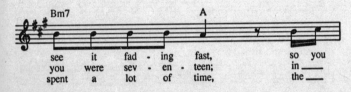

see it fad- ing fast, so you
you were sev- en- teen; in ___
spent a lot of time, the ___

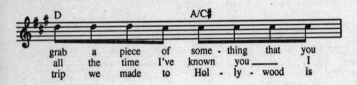

grab a piece of some- thing that you
all the time I've known you ___ I
trip we made to Hol- ly- wood is

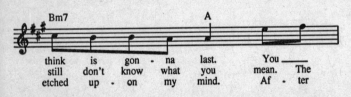

think is gon- na last. You ___ The
still don't know what you mean. The
etched up- on my mind. Af- ter

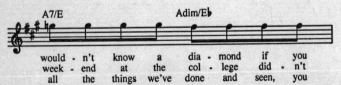

would- n't know a dia- mond if you
week- end at the col- lege did- n't
all the things we've done and seen, you

REVOLUTION

Words and Music by
JOHN LENNON and PAUL McCARTNEY

But when you talk a-bout de-struc-tion,_____
But if you want money for people with minds that hate,_____
But if you go carry-ing pictures of Chair-man Mao,_____

Don't you know that you can count me out.__
All I can tell you is, "Brother you have to wait."
You ain't going to make it with any-one an-y-how.__

Don't you know it's gon-na be____ al-right,__

al - right,____ al - right.__

(Instrumental)
You
You

3.
Al - right,__ al - right,__ al - right,__

al - right,__ al - right,__ al - right,__

al - right,__ al - right. (Instrumental)

RHIANNON

Words and Music by
STEVIE NICKS

Moderately

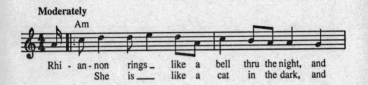

Rhi - an - non rings _ like a bell thru the night, and
She is _ like a cat in the dark, and

would - n't you love to love _ her? _
then she is the dark - ness. _

Takes to the sky like a bird in flight _ and
She rules her life like a fine sky - lark _ and

who will be _ her lov - er? }
when the sky _ is star - less. }

All your life _ you've nev - er seen _ a wom - an _

— tak - en by the wind.____

Would you stay __ if she prom - ised you heav-en?

Will you ev - er win? _____

Will you ev - er win? _____

Rhi - an -

Play 4 times

non. Dreams un - wind; love's __

Repeat and Fade

__ a state of mind. _____

ROCK AND ROLL ALL NITE

Words and Music by PAUL STANLEY
and GENE SIMMONS

Moderately

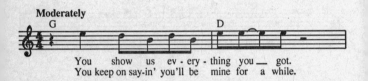

You show us ev - ery - thing you __ got.
You keep on say - in' you'll be mine for a while.

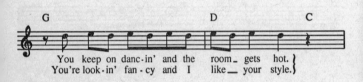

You keep on danc - in' and the room __ gets hot.
You're look - in' fan - cy and I like __ your style.

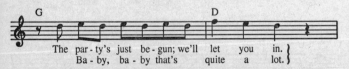

You drive us wild, __ we'll drive you cra - zy.

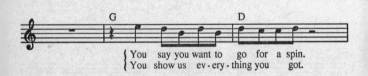

You say you want to go for a spin.
You show us ev - ery - thing you got.

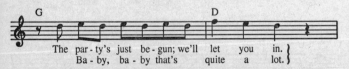

The par - ty's just be - gun; we'll let you in.
Ba - by, ba - by that's quite a lot.

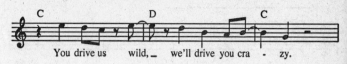

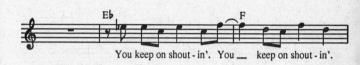

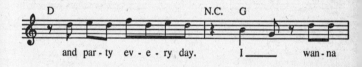

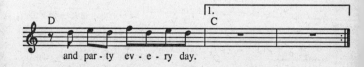

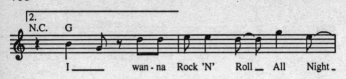

I ____ wan - na Rock 'N' Roll ____ All Night ____

____ and par - ty ev - e - ry day.

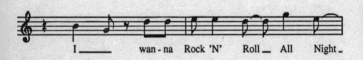

I ____ wan - na Rock 'N' Roll ____ All Night ____

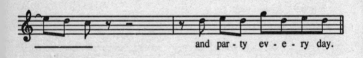

____ and par - ty ev - e - ry day.

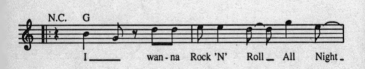

I ____ wan - na Rock 'N' Roll ____ All Night ____

Play 6 times and Fade

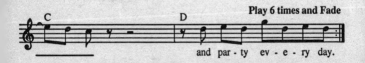

____ and par - ty ev - e - ry day.

RIKKI DON'T LOSE THAT NUMBER

Words and Music by WALTER BECKER
and DONALD FAGEN

ROCK AND ROLL
HOOCHIE KOO

Words and Music by
RICK DERRINGER

Bright rock

(Instrumental)

I
Mos-

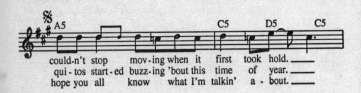

could-n't stop   mov-ing when it   first   took   hold.____
qui-tos start-ed buzz-ing 'bout this   time   of   year.____
hope you all   know   what I'm talkin'   a-bout.____

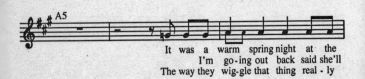

It   was a   warm spring night at the
I'm   go-ing out   back said she'll
The way they wig-gle that thing real-ly

old   town   hall.
meet   me   there.
knocks me   out.

There was a
We were
Get-tin'

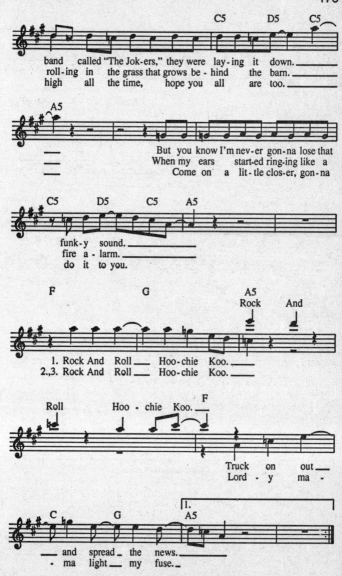

band called "The Jok-ers," they were lay-ing it down.
roll-ing in the grass that grows be-hind the barn.
high all the time, hope you all are too.

But you know I'm nev-er gon-na lose that
When my ears start-ed ring-ing like a
Come on a lit-tle clos-er, gon-na

funk-y sound.
fire a-larm.
do it to you.

1. Rock And Roll ___ Hoo-chie Koo. ___
2.,3. Rock And Roll ___ Hoo-chie Koo. ___

Roll Hoo-chie Koo. ___

Truck on out ___
Lord - y ma -

___ and spread ___ the news. ___
- ma light ___ my fuse. ___

174

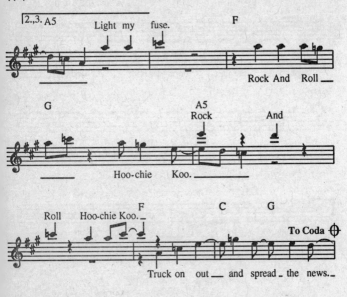

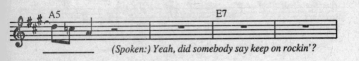

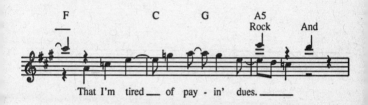

ROCK & ROLL - PART II
(THE HEY SONG)

Words and Music by GARY GLITTER
and MIKE LEANDER

ROCK'N ME

Words and Music by
STEVE MILLER

Moderate Rock beat

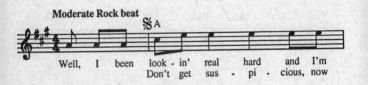

Well, I been look - in' real hard and I'm
Don't get sus - pi - cious, now

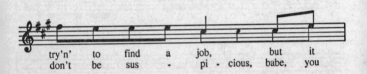

try'n' to find a job, but it
don't be sus - pi - cious, babe, you

just keeps get - tin' tough - er ev - 'ry
know you are a friend of mine. _____

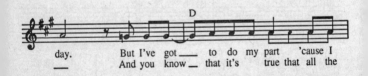

day. But I've got _____ to do my part 'cause I
_____ And you know _____ that it's true that all the

know in my heart _____ I've got to
things that I do _____ are gon - na

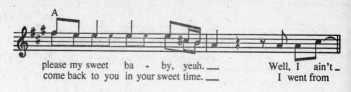

please my sweet ba - by, yeah. ___ Well, I ain't ___
come back to you in your sweet time. ___ I went from

___ su - per - sti - tious and I
Phoe - nix, Ar - i - zo - na, all the
Phoe - nix, Ar - i - zo - na, all the

don't get sus - pi - cious, 'cause my
way to Ta - co - ma, Phil - a -
way to Ta - co - ma, Phil - a -

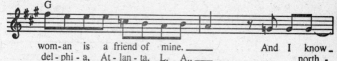

wom-an is a friend of mine. ___ And I know ___
del - phi - a, At - lan - ta, L. A., ___ north -
del - phi - a, At - lan - ta, L. A., ___ north -

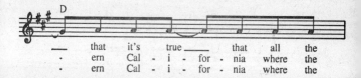

___ that it's true ___ that all the
- ern Cal - i - for - nia where the
- ern Cal - i - for - nia where the

things that I do ___ will come back ___
girls are warm ___ so I could
girls are warm ___ so I could

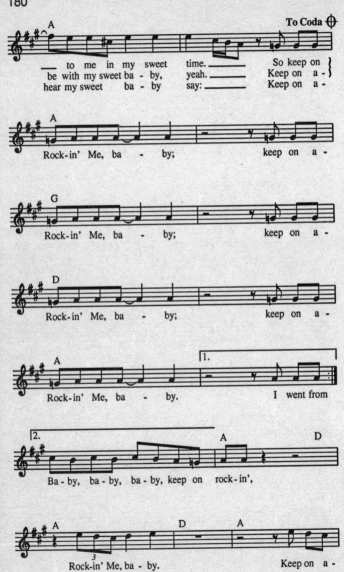

To Coda

181

ROCK THE CASBAH

Words and Music by
THE CLASH

Am7

sheik, he drove his Ca - dil - lac.
Bed - ou - in, they brought out the e -
soon as the sha - reef was

Em7

He went a -
lec - tric cam - el drum. The
chauf - fered out - ta there, the

G7

cruis - in' down the ville.
lo - cal gui - tar pick - er got his
jet pi - lots tuned to the

Dm7   Am7

The muez-zin was a stand-ing
gui - tar pick-ing thumb. As soon as the sha-reef had
cock-pit ra - dio blare. As soon as the sha-reef was

Em7   Fmaj7

on the ra - di - a - tor grille. ___
cleared the square, they be - gan to wail. ___
outta their hair, the jet pi - lots wailed. ___

Dm7   Am7 G7

Sha - reef ___ don't like it. ___

184

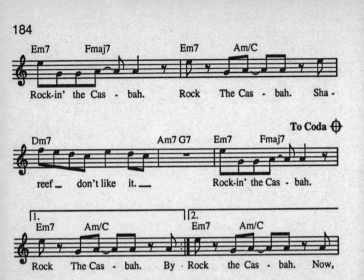

Em7   Fmaj7   Em7   Am/C

Rock-in' the Cas - bah.   Rock   The Cas - bah.   Sha -

To Coda ⊕

Dm7   Am7 G7   Em7   Fmaj7

reef __ don't like it. __   Rock-in' the Cas - bah.

1.
Em7   Am/C

2.
Em7   Am/C

Rock   The Cas - bah.   By · Rock   the Cas - bah.   Now,

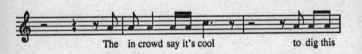

Am7

o - ver at the tem-ple,   oh, they real-ly pack 'em in.

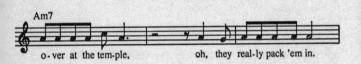

The in crowd say it's cool   to dig this

Fmaj7

chant-ing thing.   But as the wind changed di - rec - tion

G7

and the tem-ple band took five,   the

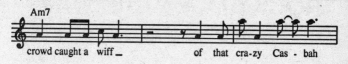

crowd caught a wiff ___ of that cra-zy Cas-bah

jive. Sha-reef ___ don't like it. ___

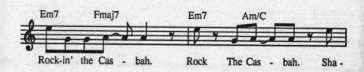

Rock-in' the Cas-bah. Rock The Cas-bah. Sha-

reef ___ don't like it. ___

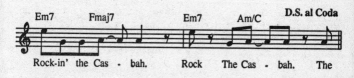

Rock-in' the Cas-bah. Rock The Cas-bah. The

Rock The Cas-bah. Sha-reef ___ don't like it. ___

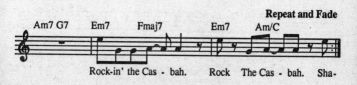

Rock-in' the Cas-bah. Rock The Cas-bah. Sha-

ROCKY MOUNTAIN WAY

Words and Music by JOE WALSH, JOE VITALE,
KEN PASSARELLI and ROCKE GRACE

Ooh, _ hoo. _ (Instrumental)

Well, he's _____

(Instrumental)

Repeat and Fade

SATURDAY NIGHT SPECIAL

Words and Music by EDWARD KING
and RONNIE VAN ZANT

Moderate Blues tempo

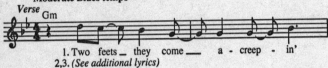

1. Two feets_ they come_ a - creep - in'
2,3. *(See additional lyrics)*

like a black cat do _

and two bod - ies are lay - in' na - ked,

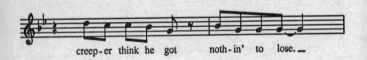

creep - er think he got noth - in' to lose. _

So, he creeps in - to _ this _ house _ *yeah!*

and un - locks _ the door. _

And as a man's reach-ing for his trou - sers,

shoots him full of thir - ty-eight holes._

Chorus
Gm

It's the Sat - ur - day Night_ Spe - cial

F   C

Got a bar - rel that's blue and cold_

Gm

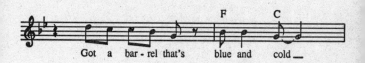

Ain't good_ for noth - in'

C

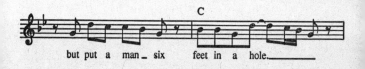

but put a man_ six feet in a hole._____

1., 2.
Gm   3.
Gm

(Instrumental)   (Instrumental)

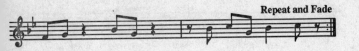

Repeat and Fade

Additional Lyrics

2. Big Jim's been drinkin' whiskey
   And playin' poker on a losin' night
   Pretty soon big Jim starts a-thinkin'
   Somebody been cheatin' and lyin'
   So big Jim commences to fightin'
   I wouldn't tell you no lie.
   And big Jim done pulled his pistol
   Shot his friend right between the eyes.

Repeat Chorus

3. Hand guns are made for killin'
   Ain't no good for nothin' else
   And if you like to drink your whiskey
   You might even shoot yourself
   So why don't we dump them people
   To the bottom of the sea.
   Before some fool come around here
   Wanna shoot either you or me.

ROXANNE

Words and Music by
STING

SHE'S SO COLD

Words and Music by MICK JAGGER
and KEITH RICHARDS

197

CODA II

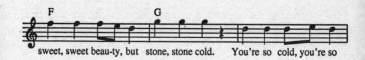
You were a beau-ty, a sweet, sweet, beau-ty, a

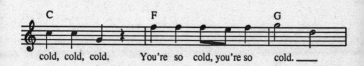
sweet, sweet beau-ty, but stone, stone cold. You're so cold, you're so

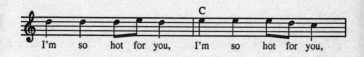
cold, cold, cold. You're so cold, you're so cold. ___

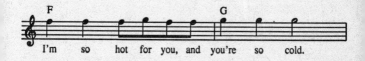
I'm so hot for you, I'm so hot for you,

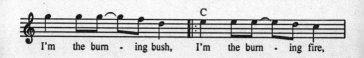
I'm so hot for you, and you're so cold.

I'm the burn - ing bush, I'm the burn - ing fire,

I'm the bleed - ing vol - ca - no.

Repeat and Fade

SPINNING WHEEL

Words and Music by
DAVID CLAYTON THOMAS

Funky, moderate Rock

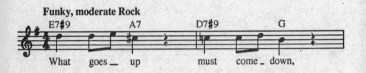

What goes up must come down,

Spin-ning Wheel got to go 'round.

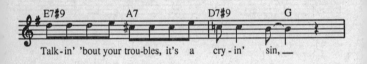

Talk-in' 'bout your trou-bles, it's a cry-in' sin,

Ride a paint-ed po-ny, let the Spin-ning Wheel spin.

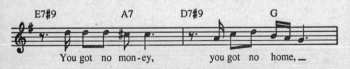

You got no mon-ey, you got no home,

Spin-ning Wheel all a - lone,

Talk-in' 'bout your trou-bles and you, you nev-er learn,

Ride a paint-ed po - ny let the Spin-ning Wheel turn.

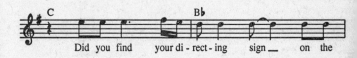

Did you find your di - rect - ing sign on the

straight and nar - row high - way?

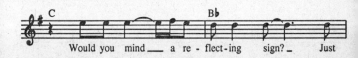

Would you mind a re - flect - ing sign? Just

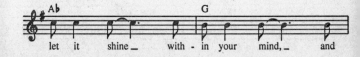

let it shine with - in your mind, and

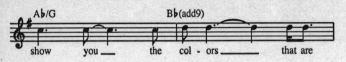

Ab/G ... Bb(add9)

show you __ the col - ors _____ that are

C(add9) ... D9

real. _____

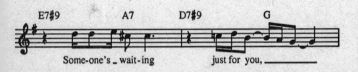

E7#9 ... A7 ... D7#9 ... G

Some-one's _ wait-ing ... just for you, _____

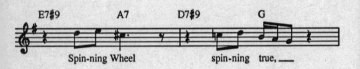

E7#9 ... A7 ... D7#9 ... G

Spin-ning Wheel ... spin-ning true, ___

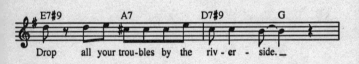

E7#9 ... A7 ... D7#9 ... G

Drop all your trou-bles by the riv - er - side. __

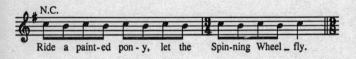

N.C.

Ride a paint-ed pon - y, let the Spin-ning Wheel _ fly.

Repeat and Fade

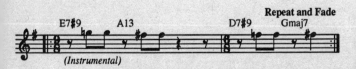

E7#9 ... A13 ... D7#9 ... Gmaj7

(Instrumental)

START ME UP

Words and Music by MICK JAGGER
and KEITH RICHARDS

SUBSTITUTE

Words and Music by
PETER TOWNSHEND

Moderately

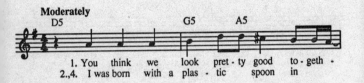

1. You think we look pret - ty good to - geth -
2.,4. I was born with a plas - tic spoon in

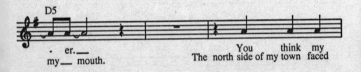

- er.   You think my
my ___ mouth.   The north side of my town faced

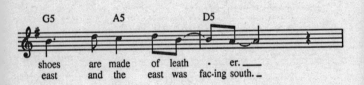

shoes   are made   of leath - er. ___
east   and the   east was   fac-ing south. __

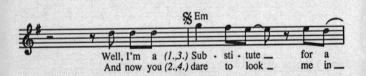

Well, I'm a (1.,3.) Sub - sti - tute ___   for a
And now you (2.,4.) dare to look ___ me in ___

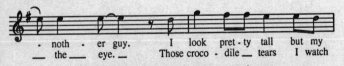

___ noth - er guy.   I look pret - ty tall   but my
___ the ___ eye. ___   Those croco - dile ___ tears   I watch

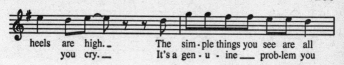

heels are high._ The sim - ple things you see are all
you cry._ It's a gen - u - ine _ prob-lem you

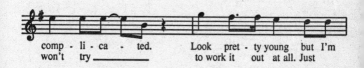

comp - li - ca - ted. Look pret - ty young but I'm
won't try _____ to work it out at all. Just

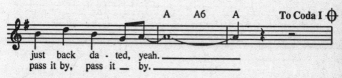

A   A6   A   To Coda I

just back da - ted, yeah. _____
pass it by, pass it _ by. _____

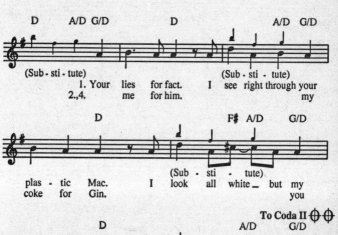

D   A/D G/D   D   A/D G/D

(Sub - sti - tute)   (Sub - sti - tute)
1. Your lies for fact.   I see right through your
2.,4,   me for him.   my

D   F♯ A/D   G/D

(Sub - sti - tute)
plas - tic Mac.   I look all white _ but my
coke for Gin.   you

To Coda II

D   A/D   G/D

(Sub - sti - tute)
dad was black._ My Si - a-mese shoes real - ly
for my mum._ At least I'll get my

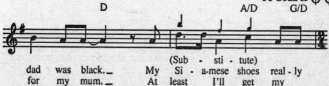

1.
made out of sack.___

wash - ing ___ done._

2.

D.S. al Coda I

Well, I'm a

CODA I Interlude

D   A   G   **1.,2.,3.**   D

4. (G)   D

D.C. al Coda II

CODA II

D   A/D   G/D

wash - ing done. _

(Sub - sti - tute)
1. Your
2. look   all   white   but my

D   D   A/D   G/D

lies   for   fact. _   I   see   right   through   your
dad   was   black. _   I   sense   these   shoes   is really

(Sub - sti - tute)

1. D   **2.** D

plast - ic   Mac. _   I

made out a' sack. _

SUFFRAGETTE CITY

Words and Music by
DAVID BOWIE

Medium beat

Hey man oh leave me a - lone, you know.

Hey man oh Hen - ry get off the phone. I got - ta

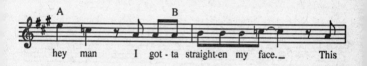

hey man I got - ta straight-en my face. This

mel-low-thighed chick just put my spine out of place.

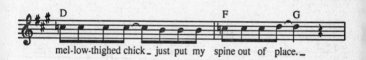

Hey man my school day's in - sane.

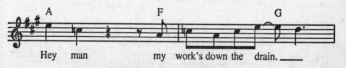

Hey man my work's down the drain.

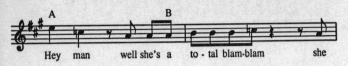

Hey man   well she's a   to - tal blam-blam   she

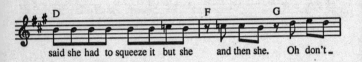

said she had to squeeze it but she   and then she.   Oh don't

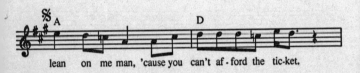

lean   on me man, 'cause you can't af-ford the tic-ket.

I'm back on Suf-fra-gette Cit - y.   No don't

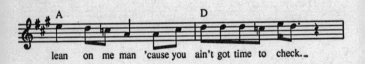

lean   on me man 'cause you ain't got time to check.

You know my Suf-fra-gette Cit - y   is ou-ta

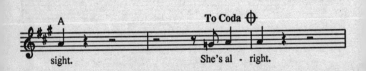

sight.   She's al - right.

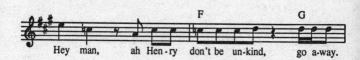

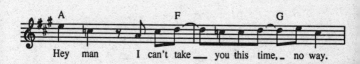
Hey man, ah Hen-ry don't be un-kind, go a-way.

Hey man I can't take ___ you this time, _ no way.

Hey man droo-gie don't crash here. ___ There's

on-ly room for one and here she comes, here she comes. _ Ah don't

CODA

right A Suf-fra-gette Ci - ty

Suf-fra - gette

THE SUNSHINE OF YOUR LOVE

Words and Music by JACK BRUCE, PETE BROWN and ERIC CLAPTON

(Instrumental)

I've __ been wait - ing so __ long

to __ be where __ I'm go - ing

in __ The Sun - shine Of __ Your

Love. _____

D.S. al Coda

(Instrumental)

I'm

212

CODA

(Instrumental)

I've __ been wait - ing so __ long,

I've __ been wait - ing __ so long. __

I've __ been wait - ing so __ long

to __ be where __ I'm go - ing

in __ The Sun - shine Of __ Your

Love. _____

SWEET HOME ALABAMA ²¹³

**Words and Music by RONNIE VAN ZANT,
ED KING and GARY ROSSINGTON**

Moderately

Big wheels keep on turn-ing

Car-ry me home to see my kin.

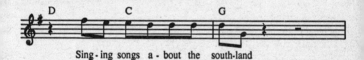

Sing-ing songs a - bout the south-land

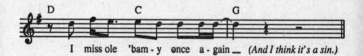

I miss ole 'bam - y once a - gain __ *(And I think it's a sin.)*

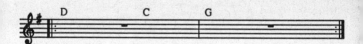

Well, I heard Mis-ter Young sing a - bout her.

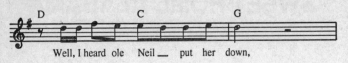

Well, I heard ole Neil __ put her down,

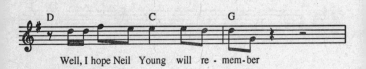

Well, I hope Neil Young will re - mem - ber

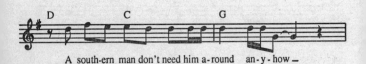

A south-ern man don't need him a-round an - y - how __

Sweet Home Al - a - bam - a,

Where the skies are so blue,

Sweet Home Al - a - bam - a,

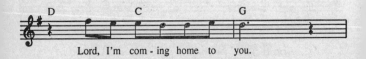

Lord, I'm com - ing home to you.

SURRENDER

Words and Music by STEVE BROWN, JIM WRAY and BILL WRAY

Rock Ballad

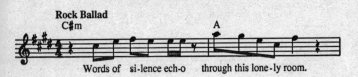

Words of si-lence ech-o through this lone-ly room.

Just a pho-to-graph and dreams

that won't come true.

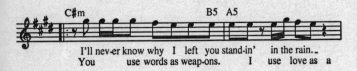

I'll nev-er know why I left you stand-in' in the rain.
You use words as weap-ons. I use love as a

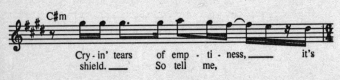

Cry-in' tears of emp-ti-ness, it's
shield. So tell me,

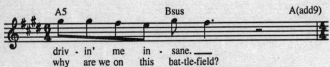

driv-in' me in-sane.
why are we on this bat-tle-field?

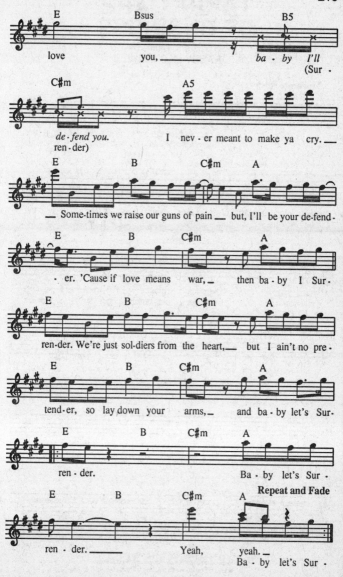

TAKIN' CARE OF BUSINESS

Words and Music by
RANDY BACHMAN

Moderate Rock

They get up ev-'ry morn-in' from the
There's work eas-y as fish-in', you could

'larm clock's warn-in', take the eight fif-teen in-to the
be a mu-si-cian if you can make sounds loud or

cit-y.   There's a whis-tle up a-bove and peo-ple
mel-low.   Get a sec-ond hand gui-tar, chanc-es

push-in', peo-ple shov-in' and the girls who try to look
are you'll go far if you get in with the right bunch of

pret-ty.   And if your train's on time, you can
fel-lows.   Peo-ple see you hav-in' fun, just a

get to work by nine, and start your slav-in' job to get your
ly-in' in the sun, tell them that you like it this

TUMBLING DICE

Words and Music by MICK JAGGER
and KEITH RICHARDS

Moderate rock

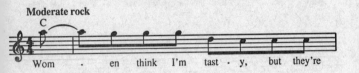

Wom - en think I'm tast - y, but they're

al - ways try - in' to waste me and make _ me burn the can - dle right down, _

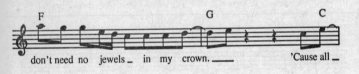

_ but ba - by, _ ba - by, _ I

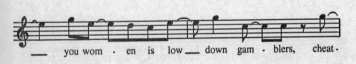

don't need no jewels _ in my crown. _ 'Cause all _

_ you wom - en is low _ down gam - blers, cheat -

- in' like I don't know how, _ but ba - by, _

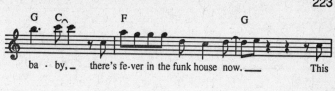

ba - by, _ there's fe-ver in the funk house now. ___ This

low down bitch-in' got my ___ poor feet a - itch-in', you know, _

___ you know the deuce is still wild. _____

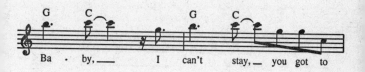

Ba - by, ___ I can't stay, _ you got to

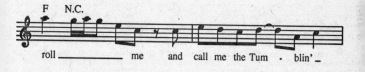

roll _____ me and call me the Tum - blin' _

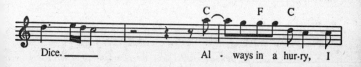

Dice. _____ Al - ways in a hur-ry, I

nev-er stop to wor-ry, don't _ you see the time _ flash-in' by. _

224

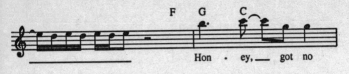

Hon · ey, ___ got no

mon · ey, ___ I'm all six · es and sev · ens and nines. ___

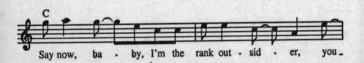

Say now, ba · by, I'm the rank out · sid · er, you ___

___ can be my part · ner in crime. ___ But

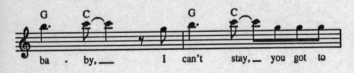

ba · by, ___ I can't stay, ___ you got to

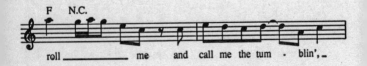

roll ___ me and call me the tum · blin', ___

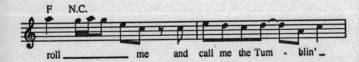

roll ___ me and call me the Tum · blin' ___

225

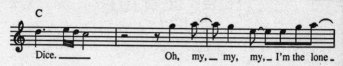

Dice. ____ Oh, my,_ my, my,_ I'm the lone-

_ crap shoot - er, play - in' the field _ ev·'ry night. __

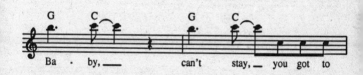

Ba - by, ___ can't stay,_ you got to

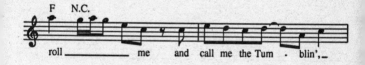

roll _____ me and call me the Tum - blin',_

roll _____ me and call me the Tum - blin' ____
(Dice. _____) (Got to

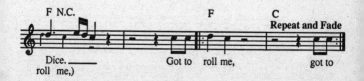

Dice.____ Got to roll me, got to
roll me,)

UNDERCOVER
(OF THE NIGHT)

Words and Music by MICK JAGGER
and KEITH RICHARDS

1. Heard the screams of Cen - tre For - ty - Two:
2.-4. *(See additional lyrics)*

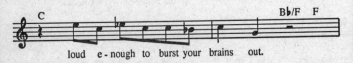

loud e - nough to burst your brains out.

1. The op - po - si - tion's tongue is ___ cut in two. __
3., 4.

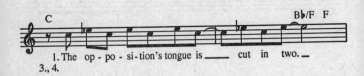

Keep off the street 'cause you're in dan - ger.

1. Four hun - dred thou - sand "dis - pa - rus",
2., 3., 4.

To Coda ⊕⊕   To Coda ⊕

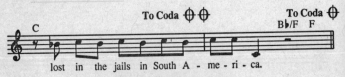

lost in the jails in South A - me - ri - ca.

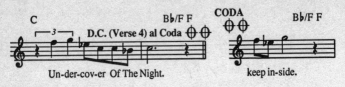

Un-der-cov-er Of The Night.   keep in-side.

Un - der - cov - er.   Keep it all out of sight.

Un-der-cov-er Of The Night.   (Vocal/Instrumental - Ad lib.)

Repeat and Fade

Additional Lyrics

2. The sex police are out there on the streets
   Make sure the Pass Laws are not broken.
   The Race Militia is got itchy fingers
   All the way from New York back to Africa.

3. All the young men, they've been rounded up
   And sent to camps back in the jungle.
   And people whisper; people double talk.
   And once proud fathers act so humble.
   All the young girls, they have got the blues.
   They're heading all back to Centre Forty-Two.

4. Down in the bars, the girls are painted blue;
   Done up in lace; done up in rubber.
   The Johns are jerky G. I. Joes
   On R & R from Cuba and Russia.
   The smell of sex; the smell of suicide.
   All these things I can't keep inside.

UP ON CRIPPLE CREEK

Words and Music by
ROBBIE ROBERTSON

Moderate funk-rock
Verse

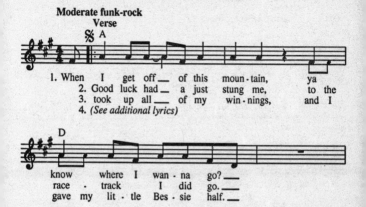

1. When I get off ___ of this moun-tain, ya
2. Good luck had ___ a just stung me, to the
3. took up all ___ of my win-nings, and I
4. *(See additional lyrics)*

know where I wan-na go? ___
race-track I did go. ___
gave my lit-tle Bes-sie half. ___

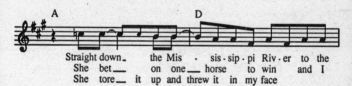

Straight down ___ the Mis-sis-sip-pi Riv-er to the
She bet ___ on one horse to win and I
She tore ___ it up and threw it in my face

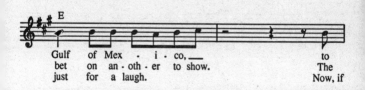

Gulf of Mex-i-co, ___ to
bet on an-oth-er to show. The
just for a laugh. Now, if

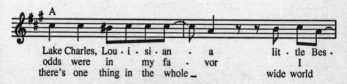

Lake Charles, Lou-i-si-an-a lit-tle Bes-
odds were in my fa-vor I
there's one thing in the whole ___ wide world

230

D
- sie girl ___ I once knew. ___
had 'em five to one.
I sure would ___ like to see, ___

A   **D**
And she told ___ me just to come on by, ___ if there's
And that nag ___ to win ___ came a-round the track,
that's when that lit - tle love ___ of mine dips her

E
an - y - thing that she could do. ___
sure e - nough, she had won. ___
do - nut in my tea.

Chorus
A
Up On Crip - ple Creek she sends me.

D
If I spring ___ a leak, she mends ___ me.

E
I don't have ___ to speak, she de - fends ___ me, a

F#m   **G**
drunk-ard's dream ___ if I ev - er did see one. ___

Additional Lyrics

4. There's a flood in California and up north, it's freezin' cold,
   and this livin' on the road is getting pretty old.
   So I guess I'll call up my big Mama, tell her I'll be rollin' in.
   But you know deep down I'm kinda tempted to go and see my Bessie again.

WALK ON THE WILD SIDE

Words and Music by
LOU REED

Moderately slow

1. Hol - ly came from Mi - a - mi F L A,
2.-5. *(See additional lyrics)*

hitch-hiked her way a - cross the U. S. A. _____

plucked her eye - brows a - long the way,

shaved her legs _____ and then he was a she, she says,

"Hey babe, take a Walk On The Wild Side, _____ said

hey babe, take a Walk On The Wild Side." And the col-ored girls go

234

Repeat and Fade

Additional Lyrics

2. Candy came from out on the Island
   In the backroom she was everybody's darling
   But she never lost her head even when she was giving head -
   the colored girls go
   Doo do doo do doo

3. Little Joe never once gave it away
   Everybody had to pay and pay
   A hustle here and a hustle there
   New York City is the place where they say
   Hey babe, take a Walk On The Wild Side

4. The Sugar Plum Fairy came and he hit the streets
   Lookin' for soul food and a place to eat.
   Went to the Apollo
   You should have seen 'em go go go

5. Jackie is just speeding away
   Thought she was James Dean for a day
   Then I guess she had to crash
   Valium would have helped that bash

   Hey take a Walk On The Wild Side
   And the colored girls go doo do doo do doo

WALK THIS WAY

Words and Music by STEVEN TYLER
and JOE PERRY

Steady

Well, there's a 1. back seat lov-er that's
2., 4. See-saw swing-er with the
3. School girl sweet-ies with a

al - ways un - der cov - er and I
boys in the school, and your
class - y, kind - a sass - y lit - tle

talked to my dad, he say, ___ he said, "You
feet fly-in' up in the air, ___ sing-in'
skirts climb-in' way up their knees; ___ there was ___

ain't seen noth-in' till you're down on a muf-fin and you're
"Hey diddle did-dle" with your kitty in the mid-dle of the
three young la-dies in the school gym ___ lock-er when I

sure to be chang-in' your ways." ___ I met a
swing ___ like you did-n't ___ care. So I
found ___ they were look-in' at me. ___ I was a

cheer - lead - er was a real big bleed-er; oh, the
took a big chance ___ at the high school dance ___ with a
high school los - er, nev - er made it with a la-dy till the

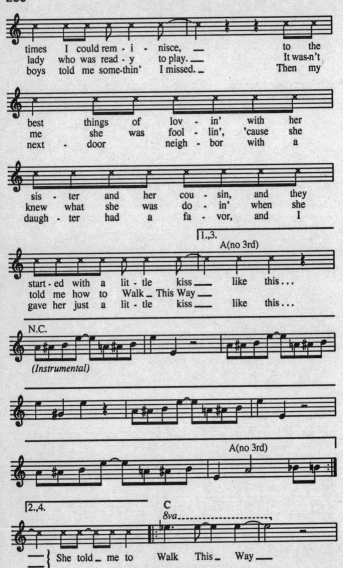

times I could rem - i - nisce, __ to the
lady who was read - y to play. __ It was-n't
boys told me some-thin' I missed. __ Then my

best things of lov - in' with her
me she was fool - in', 'cause she
next - door neigh - bor with a

sis - ter and her cou - sin, and they
knew what she was do - in' when she
daugh - ter had a fa - vor, and I

1.,3.
A(no 3rd)

start - ed with a lit - tle kiss __ like this . . .
told me how to Walk __ This Way __
gave her just a lit - tle kiss __ like this . . .

N.C.

(Instrumental)

A(no 3rd)

2.,4.
C
8va

__ } She told __ me to Walk This __ Way __

talk this _ way. _   Walk This _ Way, _

talk this _ way. _   { She told _ me to
                        { Just give _ me a

kiss   *(Instrumental)*

like this!

To Coda ⊕
A(no 3rd)   N.C.

1.

2.
D.S. al Coda
(with repeats)   CODA ⊕
A(no 3rd)   N.C.

Repeat and Fade
A(no 3rd)

WE ARE THE CHAMPIONS

Words and Music by
FREDDIE MERCURY

239

WE WILL ROCK YOU

Words and Music by
BRIAN MAY

Moderately

4 times

(Hand clap)
N.C.

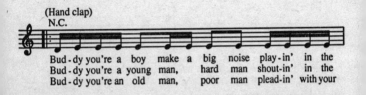

Bud - dy you're a boy make a big noise play - in' in the
Bud - dy you're a young man, hard man shout - in' in the
Bud - dy you're an old man, poor man plead - in' with your

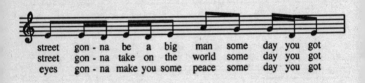

street gon - na be a big man some day you got
street gon - na take on the world some day you got
eyes gon - na make you some peace some day you got

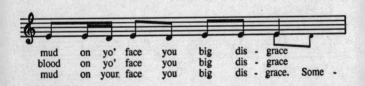

mud on yo' face you big dis - grace
blood on yo' face you big dis - grace
mud on your face you big dis - grace. Some -

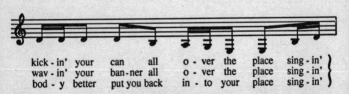

kick - in' your can all o - ver the place sing - in' }
wav - in' your ban - ner all o - ver the place sing - in'
bod - y better put you back in - to your place sing - in' }

A WHITER SHADE
OF PALE

Words and Music by KEITH REID
and GARY BROOKER

We skipped the light — fan-dan-go. _____
She said, "I'm home — on shore leave." _____

Turned cart-wheels — 'cross the floor, _
Though in truth we _____ were at sea, _____

I was feel-ing kind of sea-sick
So I took her by the looking glass

The crowd called — out for more The
And forced her _____ to _____ a-gree

243

WILD THING

Words and Music by
CHIP TAYLOR

© 1965 (Renewed 1993) EMI BLACKWOOD MUSIC INC.

I love you.
You move me.

Wild Thing.

you make my heart sing.

You make ev - 'ry - thing ___ groov - y, ___

Wild Thing.

Wild Thing.

D.C. al Coda

CODA

Repeat ad lib. and Fade

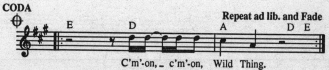

C'm'-on, _ c'm'-on, Wild Thing.

YOU AIN'T SEEN NOTHIN' YET

Words and Music by
RANDY BACHMAN

YOU MAKE LOVIN' FUN

Words and Music by
CHRISTINE McVIE

Moderate Rock beat

Gm

Sweet, _____ won-der-ful you.
_____ don't break the spell.

F

You make me hap - py with the things you do. __
It would be dif - f'rent, and you know it will. __

Eb   Gm

Oh, _____
You, _____

can it be so?
You Make Lov - ing Fun.

F

This feel - ing fol - lows me wher - ev - er I go. __
And I don't have __ to tell you you're the on - ly __

To Coda ⊕

Eb   Bb

I nev - er did be -
one.

lieve _____ in __ mir - a - cles. _____

Gm7　　　F　　　Eb
But I've a feel-ing it's time to try. __

Bb
I nev-er did be - lieve _____

Bb/Ab
__ in the ways of mag - ic.

Gm7　　　F
But I'm be - gin-ning to won - der why. __

Eb　　　D.S. al Coda　　　CODA　　Bb
Don't, _　　　You, _____

F　　　Eb　　Repeat and Fade
__ You Make _ Lov-ing Fun. __

YOU REALLY GOT ME

Words and Music by
RAY DAVIES

GUITAR CHORD FRAMES

	C	Cm	C+	C6	Cm6
C		3fr			

	C#	C#m	C#+	C#6	C#m6
C#/Db		4fr		3fr	2fr

	D	Dm	D+	D6	Dm6
D					

	Eb	Ebm	Eb+	Eb6	Ebm6
Eb/D#	3fr		× ○○×		

	E	Em	E+	E6	Em6
E					

	F	Fm	F+	F6	Fm6
F					

This guitar chord reference includes 120 commonly used
chords. For a more complete guide to guitar chords, see
"THE PAPERBACK CHORD BOOK" (HL00702009).

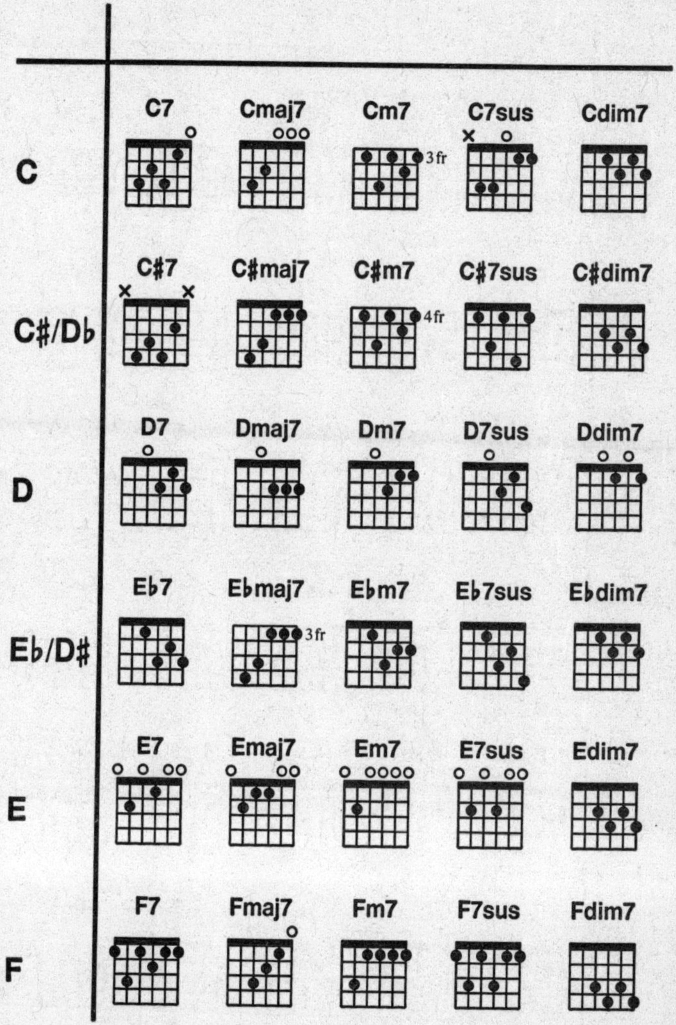
C
C7
Cmaj7
Cm7
3fr
C7sus
Cdim7
C♯/D♭
C♯7
C♯maj7
C♯m7
4fr
C♯7sus
C♯dim7
D
D7
Dmaj7
Dm7
D7sus
Ddim7
E♭/D♯
E♭7
E♭maj7
3fr
E♭m7
E♭7sus
E♭dim7
E
E7
Emaj7
Em7
E7sus
Edim7
F
F7
Fmaj7
Fm7
F7sus
Fdim7

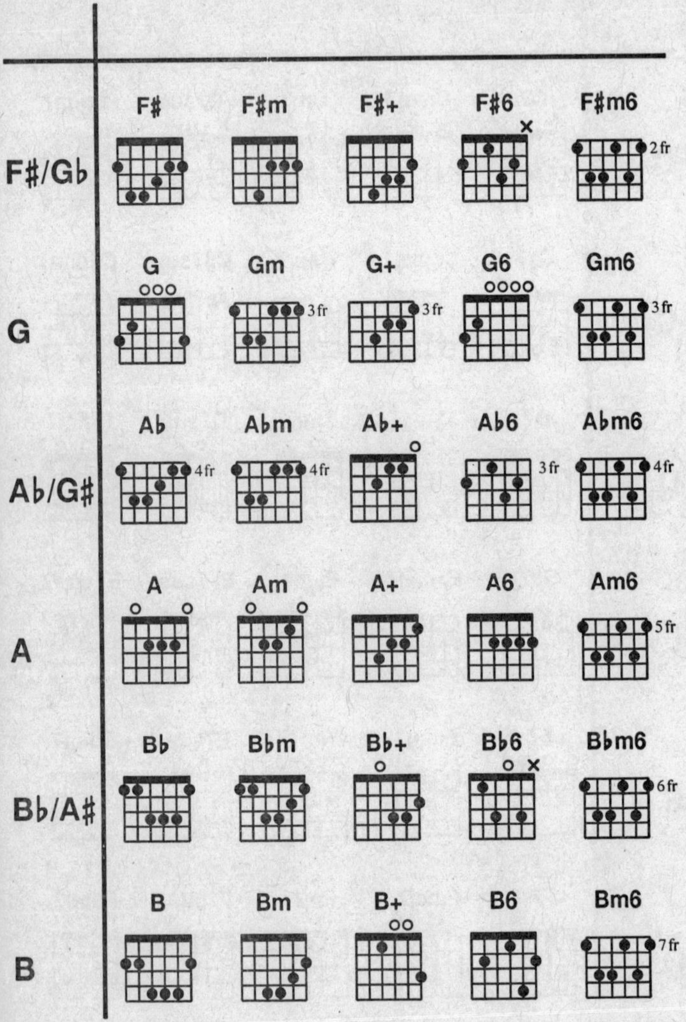
F#/Gb
F# F#m F#+ F#6 F#m6
2 fr
G
G Gm G+ G6 Gm6
3 fr 3 fr 3 fr
Ab/G#
Ab Abm Ab+ Ab6 Abm6
4 fr 4 fr 3 fr 4 fr
A
A Am A+ A6 Am6
5 fr
Bb/A#
Bb Bbm Bb+ Bb6 Bbm6
6 fr
B
B Bm B+ B6 Bm6
7 fr

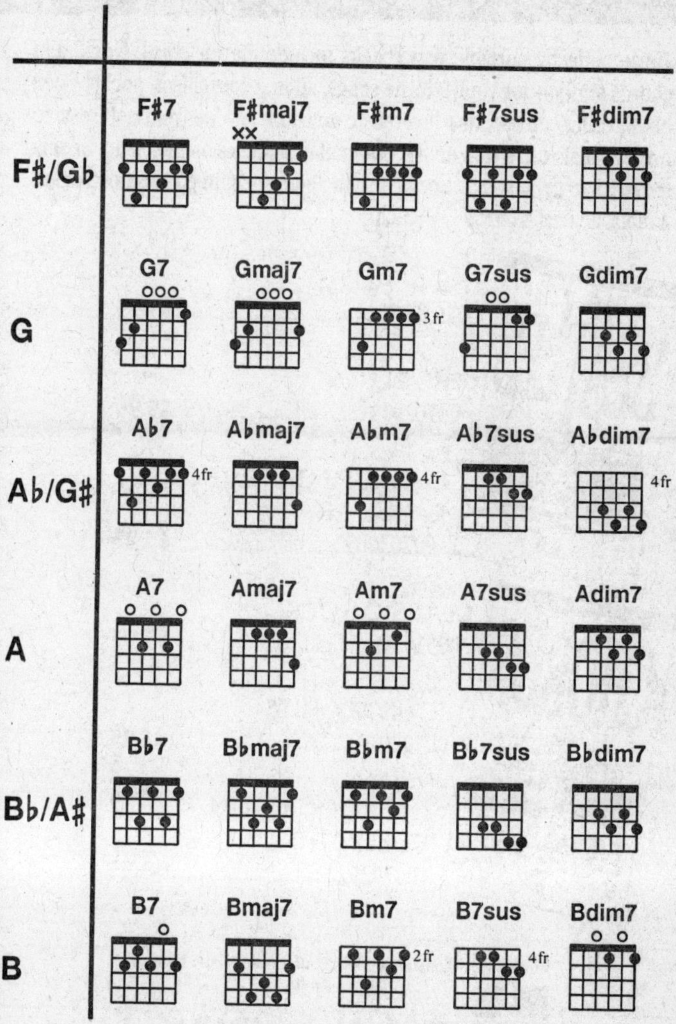

Guitar chord diagrams arranged in a grid.

Row F#/Gb: F#7, F#maj7 (××), F#m7, F#7sus, F#dim7

Row G: G7 (○○○), Gmaj7 (○○○), Gm7 (3 fr), G7sus (○○), Gdim7

Row Ab/G#: Ab7 (4 fr), Abmaj7, Abm7 (4 fr), Ab7sus, Abdim7 (4 fr)

Row A: A7 (○ ○ ○), Amaj7, Am7 (○ ○ ○), A7sus, Adim7

Row Bb/A#: Bb7, Bbmaj7, Bbm7, Bb7sus, Bbdim7

Row B: B7 (○), Bmaj7, Bm7 (2 fr), B7sus (4 fr), Bdim7 (○ ○)

THE PAPERBACK SONGS SERIES

These perfectly portable paperbacks include the melodies, lyrics, and chords symbols for your favorite songs, all in a convenient, pocket-sized book. Using concise, one-line music notation, anyone from hobbyists to professionals can strum on the guitar, play melodies on the piano, or sing the lyrics to great songs. Books also include a helpful guitar chord chart. A fantastic deal - only $5.95 each!

THE BEATLES
00702008 ....$5.95

THE BLUES
00702014 ....$5.95

CHORDS FOR KEYBOARD & GUITAR
00702009 ....$5.95

CLASSIC ROCK
00310058 ....$5.95

COUNTRY HITS
00702013 ....$5.95

THE ROCK & ROLL COLLECTION
00702020 ....$5.95

For More Information, See Your Local Music Dealer,
Or Write To:

HAL•LEONARD™
CORPORATION

7777 W. Bluemound Rd. P.O. Box 13819 Milwaukee, WI 53213

Prices, availability and contents subject to change without notice.
Some products may not be available outside the U.S.A.